Barcode in Back

MW01122008

∧

GIVE VOICE

GIVE VOICE

TEN TWENTY-MINUTE PLAYS FROM THE OBSIDIAN THEATRE COMPANY PLAYWRIGHTS UNIT

EDITED BY
RITA SHELTON DEVERELL

PLAYWRIGHTS CANADA PRESS
TORONTO

Playwrights Canada Press
The Canadian Drama Publisher
215 Spadina Ave., Suite 230, Toronto, ON Canada M5T 2C7
phone 416.703.0013 fax 416.408.3402
info@playwrightscanada.com • www.playwrightscanada.com

Playwrights Canada Press acknowledges the financial support of the Government of Canada through the Canada Book Fund and the Canada Council for the Arts and the Province of Ontario through the Ontario Arts Council and the Ontario Media Development Corporation for our publishing activities.

 Canada Council for the Arts Conseil des Arts du Canada 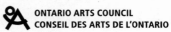 ONTARIO ARTS COUNCIL CONSEIL DES ARTS DE L'ONTARIO

 Canadä   Ontario Ontario Media Development Corporation

Cover art and design by Shelton Deverell
Type design by Blake Sproule

Library and Archives Canada Cataloguing in Publication

Give voice : ten plays from the Obsidian Theatre Company's Playwrights Unit / Rita Shelton Deverell, editor.

ISBN 978-0-88754-969-4

1. Canadian drama (English)--Black Canadian authors. 2. Canadian drama (English)--21st century. I. Deverell, Rita Shelton, 1945- II. Obsidian Theatre Company. Playwrights Unit

PS8307.G59 2011 C812'.6080896071 C2011-900637-5

First edition: February 2011
Printed and bound in Canada by AGMV Marquis, Montreal

To those who Give Voice, Space, and Encouragement.
Obsidian is jet-black volcanic glass, hard as granite.
Obsidian Theatre Company is just as strong.

TABLE OF CONTENTS

III INTRODUCTION

FAMILIES
IN THEIR MANY SHAPES AND COLOURS

3 THE BIG MESS BY EDWIGE JEAN-PIERRE
35 DAUGHTER'S LAST SUPPER BY REBECCA FISSEHA
63 HOW DO I FORGIVE MY DYING FATHER
BY LAURENCE ANTHONY

RELATIONSHIPS
IN THEIR UPS AND DOWNS

87 LATE BY MARCIA JOHNSON
109 BUS STOP BY DIAN MARIE BRIDGE
119 GROUP BY AISHA SASHA JOHN
137 THE COOKIE BY ROSEMARIE STEWART

SOCIAL ISSUES
TOO TOUGH TO IGNORE

157 EXIT VELOCITY BY RITA SHELTON DEVERELL
181 ANEEMAH'S SPOT/THE BASE
BY MOTION (AKA WENDY BRAITHWAITE)
209 BRIDGE OVER JOAN BY RACHAEL-LEA RICKARDS

INTRODUCTION

"The Underground Railroad doesn't have to be our only subject!" rants Philip Akin, Obsidian Theatre Company's artistic director, as he lectures the members of the Playwrights Unit in one of his favourite pep talks.

Philip is serious, and the plays created at Obsidian Theatre's Playwrights Unit are proof that playwrights are at the heart of Obsidian's mandate: "Our threefold mission is to produce plays, to develop playwrights and to train emerging theatre professionals," proclaims the website of Canada's Black-focused theatre.

The theatre was founded in the first year of this new millennium by Philip Akin and twelve other theatre artists of colour, all of whom continually make names for themselves at Obsidian and in the "mainstream" of Canadian theatre on larger stages.

If the end goal was completely about working in the mainstream, and the founders have made it there, then why a need for a Black-focused theatre? Specifically, why the need for a Playwrights Unit?

The answer is that theatre people need to have places to constantly create their work and that such places have been few and far between for visible-minority players. As well, there is a need to have a Canadian national Black theatre that welcomes other marginalized theatre artists and develops and preserves its canon. The word-makers, the playwrights, are key to there being such a vibrant theatre.

To be a part of the Playwrights Unit is also to experience the dictionary definition of "obsidian," the volcanic glass: jet-black, chemically similar to granite, formed by the rapid cooling of molten lava, used by early civilizations for manufacturing tools and ceremonial objects.

My first year in the Playwrights Unit was 2007–2008. The other members from that year and I were designing tools and ceremonial objects. We wished our words to last as long as granite. And we lived through, and were challenged by, the jet-black volcanic glass, the mirrors to the souls of our colleagues, and artistic director Akin.

Obsidian Theatre, states the company's mandate, "was born out of a passionate sense of artistic responsibility—a responsibility to bring the Black voice, in its many artistic dialects, to Canada's cultural forefront. Obsidian encourages Black artists to expand their vision of what they perceive, create and present to a national audience. Obsidian continues to play a prominent role in Canada's theatrical mosaic by showcasing the work of both emerging and established Black artists."

We hope this book will be as much of a treat for you as sitting around the table in the Playwrights Unit was for us. Each of the unit's four years have been a "venue for exploration, vision and freedom from the constraints of community or self-censorship. We believe that Black stories are and should be about anything we put our vision to," concludes Obsidian's mandate.

Playwrights must be committed to the unit because we have to make up for a lot of lost time when there have been few places for us, our work, our words, and our issues. And in theatre everything starts when those words are allowed to be given flesh.

The death of Lena Horne in 2010, the first African-American woman to sign a long-term contract with a major studio (MGM) in 1943 causes me to pause once again over the key role of he/she who creates the words. For visible-minority players there may be literally no platform from which their words will be heard. Horne, an acclaimed, dazzling performer, had the problem of never having quite enough of the right words written for her. She wasn't a playwright, and even if she had been she was born fifty years too early to have a stage. Ms. Horne wasn't Black enough, or White enough, and there were no scripts where she could be the "star" she so clearly was. Had Horne not been a person of colour there would have been countless scripts for her to star in over her sixty-year career. Finally, after she was an old woman, all of those missed opportunities were turned her into two-time Tony Award winner of a Broadway hit, a one-woman, one-of-a-kind show starring Lena Horne.

We can all be grateful to Philip Akin for putting a portion of the limited resources of Obsidian Theatre into developing playwrights, without whom there is no Black voice. We do need to build our own theatrical tools and have the opportunity to continually use them.

This book contains work from the three years since the Obsidian Playwrights Unit was started in 2006–07. The twenty-minute scripts of this volume are just some of the results of the constant coaching, freedom, and support we were given. At the end of each season Obsidian devotes some of its financial resources to staged readings with skilled professional actors and directors. The readings are standing-room only events. Why? Because they are one of the few opportunities to see and hear new works, in the many artistic Black dialects, beautifully presented.

I've grouped the ten scripts in this book by theme, but each play has many other themes, issues, and reasons for you to read, share, and enjoy. First, three scripts that get inside the lives and heads of families. These families are of different shapes, sizes, and colours. They are functional, dysfunctional, quirky, tragic, funny, and extended. Next we move on to four plays that let us experience troubled and troublesome relationships. Who chooses whom? Is it all random? What happens when the one we love to adore or love to hate removes themselves from our world? Finally, we dive into three plays about contemporary social issues, where the personal is political and the political is personal. These scripts chronicle the lives of the marginalized and the dispossessed, who have made unusual life choices, and who try to find their own solutions.

Following each play is a short biographical note about each playwright. They have been asked to share their proudest achievements, their sources of inspiration, and what they both love and hate about writing plays. Most importantly each of them have weighed in with their own thoughts of the role Obsidian Theatre has played in their own development and to the world of Canadian theatre.

One of my mentors said, "To succeed you need two things: talent and opportunity." We are each largely responsible for nurturing our own talents. Obsidian Theatre Company gives opportunity to those who are frequently denied it by more established cultural institutions, and for that we are grateful. Plus we had fun.

These twenty-minute plays are ideal for a high-school or university class session. Any three can create a full-length theatrical evening. There are a tremendous range of voices—Black voices—and styles.

When Obsidian Theatre does a public reading of the plays written in the Playwrights Unit with professional actors and directors, it is called the Mussorgsky Project. Why Mussorgsky you may ask? Because like the composer's "Pictures in the Hallway," these short scripts were triggered by visual arts, paintings, photographs, and sculptures. However, I will leave it to the playwrights to tell you about that in their own words.

Yes, there is a lot more here than memories of the Underground Railroad. There is humour, tears, joy, and the complex slaveries that ripple through individuals, families, communities, cities, and history.

Rita Shelton Deverell
Halifax, 2010

FAMILIES
IN THEIR MANY SHAPES AND COLOURS

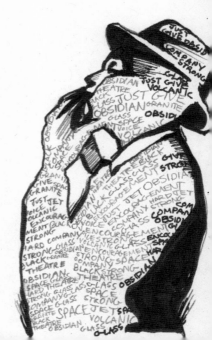

THE BIG MESS
BY EDWIGE JEAN-PIERRE

voice give just granite company black theatre
OBSIDIAN ENCOURAGEMENT GLASS STRONG JET
SPACE VOICE GIVE JUST GRANITE COMPANY BLACK
THEATRE OBSIDIAN ENCOURAGEMENT GLASS
HARD STRONG SPACE JET VOICE GIVE JUST
GRANITE COMPANY BLACK THEATRE
OBSIDIAN ENCOURAGEMENT GLASS SPAC

CHARACTERS

Fiona Waddington: In grade eight. She's the only child of Susan and Daniel Waddington. After witnessing her parents arguing for the first time, she suspects that they are splitting up. She's the follower in her clique.

Daniel Waddington: He is in his early forties. Father of Fiona Waddington and husband of Susan Waddington.

Susan Waddington: She is in her early forties. Mother of Fiona Waddington and wife of Daniel Waddington.

Valerie Cooper: In grade eight. She's Fiona's best friend and Scott's girlfriend. She's very extroverted, opinionated, and tends to jump prematurely to conclusions. Her parents are separated.

Jake Belvedere: In grade eight. He is Scott's best friend. The class clown. He seems to be coping with his parents' recent divorce. He's a latchkey kid.

Scott Mason: In grade eight. He is Valerie's boyfriend and Jake's best friend. His parents are divorced but somehow feels that he is responsible for their breakup. He's desperately trying to make it up to them by being the perfect son.

Chorus: The chorus consists of Valerie, Jake, Scott, and Fiona. Whoever is singing lead in a song is not part of the chorus. Except for "Entirely For You," where everyone is singing.

SCENE 1

Sunday night. A family of three is sitting at a dining table. SUSAN and DANIEL are sitting at both ends. FIONA is sitting in the middle. They are eating their dinner in silence.

SUSAN   Can you pass the salt?

DANIEL   Here you go.

SUSAN   Thank you.

They continue eating in silence. FIONA is playing with her food. She's observing her parents without saying a word.

Stop playing with your food, Fiona.

FIONA sighs and without an appetite resumes eating her dinner. She puts her fork on the table.

FIONA   Can I go now? I'm not hungry anymore.

DANIEL   All right, kiddo.

SUSAN looks at DANIEL in disbelief.

SUSAN   No, you are going to stay at this table and finish your dinner.

DANIEL   She said she's not hungry. Give her a break!

FIONA	Can I go now?
SUSAN	Fine.

FIONA runs to her room. She calls her best friend VALERIE. We hear SUSAN and DANIEL arguing in the background.

Why do I always have to be the bad guy? You know she's going to be hungry in a few hours.

DANIEL	Who said you were the bad guy? I know what this is about. It's about the lettuce, isn't it? Isn't it?!
SUSAN	*(whispering)* Dan, please keep your voice down.
FIONA	Hi Mrs. Cooper, is Valerie there? Thank you.
VALERIE	Hey Fifi, what's up?
FIONA	Don't call me that!
VALERIE	Sorry. What's up?
FIONA	Not much.

We hear SUSAN and DANIEL arguing.

DANIEL	Fine!
SUSAN	Fine!
VALERIE	Whoa! What was that?
FIONA	My parents. It sucks big time.
VALERIE	I know what you mean. My parents fought all the time. Now they're separated. Don't be surprised if they drop the D-bomb on you.

DANIEL picks up the phone and starts dialling.

FIONA   I'm on the phone! I'm on the phone! I'M ON THE   PHH-
HOOOONNNNEEEEE!

DANIEL   Fiona, I need the phone.

FIONA sighs.

VALERIE   Hi Mr. Waddington.

DANIEL   Hello Valerie. Finish it up, girls, I need the phone.

FIONA   *(She sighs.)* Fine!

They all stay on the line without saying anything.

DANIEL   Goodbye Valerie, Fiona will see you tomorrow at school.

VALERIE   Uhhh… Goodbye Mr. Waddington. See you tomorrow, Ona.

FIONA   Bye. Are you happy now, Dad?

DANIEL   Ona? Is that a new nickname?

FIONA   Never mind. *(She hangs up the phone.)*

SCENE 2

Monday. FIONA is eating lunch with her friends in the school's cafeteria.

VALERIE   So, Ona, how did it go last night?

FIONA   Uhh… I don't know… Okay, I guess.

VALERIE	D-bomb… It's coming… it's coming. *(She smiles at her and pats her on the back.)*
FIONA	Don't look too sad about it. Jeez!
VALERIE	Come on, it's not that bad.
FIONA	Oh yeah? Really?
VALERIE	It's not as bad as you think. You won't have to listen to your parents fight all the time. When my parents split up, I was so relieved because for once in a very long time I knew there would be some peace and quiet in our house. *(pause)* It's no big deal.
FIONA	Maybe a separation would be okay, I guess. I don't want them to get divorced.
VALERIE	I hear ya.
FIONA	Lerie, what's the difference between a divorce and a separation?
VALERIE	Okay, this is what my Uncle Max, who happens to be a lawyer, told me. Basically, a divorce is finalized and your parents are no longer married. Like it's final, like uhh… it's for real, know what I mean? Anyway, your mom can pay extra money and go back to her maiden name. And when you're separated *(in an unconvincing cheerful tone)* it's just that! You don't live together, you're separated but the woman still carries the guy's last name. He told me that if my parents are separated for seven years straight then they are legally divorced. So that means they can marry someone else. It's pretty simple!
FIONA	Things are never the same. Everything changes. Your whole life changes and there's nothing you can do about it. Nothing.

VALERIE	That's where you're wrong, Ona... Things don't have to change if you don't want them to. If they're separated you have seven years to work on getting your parents back together. *(thinking out loud)* Just have to think of how I'm going to do that. It'll be five years, ten months, two weeks, and three days tomorrow. God, five years, ten months, two weeks, and three days tomorrow! What am I going to do?
FIONA	What are you going to do?
VALERIE	I don't know. I mean, I cut classes, talk back to my parents to get their attention. At least it gives them something to talk about. If I don't see any results soon I'm gonna have to start hanging out with the "bad crowd."
FIONA	What? You're gonna start hanging out with Roxanne and her gang of troublemakers?
VALERIE	It's not definite for sure. I'm weighing my options. Jeez, Ona, relax. You wouldn't understand.
FIONA	Explain. I'm not stupid, you know, I—
JAKE	Look around you, Waddington, all our parents have split up. You're the only one whose parents are still together. You're like *The Last Unicorn.*
SCOTT	Yeah, you're the last one.
VALERIE	I hope your parents won't fight over you for custody. Scott says it's a pain in the ass.
SCOTT	The absolute worst.
FIONA	You think my parents are gonna split up?
VALERIE	I don't want to be a downer but it kinda looks like it.

FIONA	*(She feels saddened by the news.)* Oh. *(She sighs.)*
VALERIE	You're not alone, Ona, we've all been there.

> *The school bell rings. Everyone exits except for* FIONA, *who remains seated at the table.*

FIONA'S SONG

FIONA	She's walking around with this frown on her face
	Her folks are splitting up
	She looks straight at me with this real sad look
	Says I'm next
	I wake up at nights
	A sigh of relief this is only a dream
	They say that life will make much more sense with age
	Mom and Dad please don't split up
	I'm so afraid of where we'll end up
	I don't want to be a latchkey kid like my friend Jake
	Mom and Dad please don't split up
	I'm so afraid of where we'll end up
	This is causing me to suffer from a bellyache
	I have to stay cool for Pete's sake
	I walk in the caf, here comes the unicorn
CHORUS	Ha! Ha! Ha! Ha! Ha! Ha! Ha!
FIONA	They're looking at me as if I'm from outer space
CHORUS	Ha! Ha! Ha! Ha! Ha! Ha! Ha!
FIONA	I wake up at nights
	A sigh of relief, this is only a dream
	They say that life will make much more sense with age

Mom and Dad don't you split up
The kids at school
Say that our time as a tight-knit family is almost up
Mom and Dad don't you split up
I'm so afraid of where we'll end up
I'm afraid of where you'll end up
I'm afraid of where I'll end up
Better play cool
So shape up

> FIONA *takes her backpack and exits.*

SCENE 3

> *In the evening, back at the Waddington dining table.* SUSAN, DANIEL, *and* FIONA *are quietly eating their dinner.*

SUSAN How was your day, kiddo?

FIONA Fine.

SUSAN Good.

DANIEL Hey "Ona," can you pass me the pepper? *(FIONA rolls her eyes.)*

FIONA Here Dad. Can you not call me that please?

SUSAN Anything exciting happen today at school?

FIONA Not really.

DANIEL Well what did you do today?

FIONA Reading, writing, math, French, and geography.

DANIEL Okay then...

They eat in silence.

FIONA   What about you guys? Anything exciting happen today?

SUSAN   Well, you know, the usual. *(SUSAN makes a faint smile and looks at DANIEL.)*

DANIEL Yeah, just the usual... *(DANIEL smiles back at SUSAN.)*

FIONA   Anything else?

SUSAN   No, just work.

FIONA   Oh, okay then...

DANIEL Is everything all right?

FIONA   Yeah, everything's cool, Dad. I'm done, can I go now?

SUSAN   Yeah okay.

FIONA exits the room.

DANIEL Did Fiona seem all right to you tonight?

SUSAN   She's just going through stuff. She's a teenager... When do you think we should tell her?

DANIEL I think... Uh... Sometime next week, maybe? What do you think?

SUSAN   Sounds good to me.

DANIEL I got you something.

SUSAN   What? What did you get me?

DANIEL Close your eyes.

SUSAN closes her eyes. DANIEL quietly opens the refrigerator door and takes a little salad bowl out.

No peeking.

SUSAN   I'm not.

DANIEL puts the salad bowl on the table.

DANIEL   Okay, you can look now.

SUSAN opens her eyes and looks at the bowl. She's touched.

SUSAN   Boston?

DANIEL   Boston.

SUSAN   I love you.

DANIEL   I love you too.

SUSAN kisses DANIEL. They resume eating their dinner.

SCENE 4

The next day at school. FIONA is eating lunch with JAKE in the school's cafeteria.

JAKE   Hey unicorn! What's up? Did you have the "talk" yet?

FIONA   No. I tried to get them to spill the beans but it didn't work.

VALERIE arrives at the table with SCOTT.

VALERIE   Hey Ona!

FIONA   Hey Lerie!

She exchanges an inquiring look to JAKE. JAKE *looks back at her and shakes his head.*

VALERIE   No news, eh?

FIONA   Nope.

          SCOTT *takes out his geography test from his backpack and slams it on the table*

SCOTT   I got an A+ on my geography test! Yes! Yes! Yeah baby!

FIONA   You're such a brainiac, Scott.

SCOTT   It's not like I wanna be a total nerd. I've got no choice.

          I have to do well. I gotta have good grades. I just gotta, Fiona. I just gotta.

Scott's Song

SCOTT   I gotta be good
          I gotta be strong
          I gotta make sure I do well in school
          I gotta be good
          I gotta be strong
          I gotta make sure I make the team
          I gotta be good
          I gotta be strong
          I gotta make sure I like my new dad—for my mom's sake
          I gotta be good

CHORUS   Gotta be good

SCOTT   I gotta be strong

CHORUS   Gotta be strong

SCOTT	I gotta keep in touch with my real dad I gotta be good I gotta be strong I have to make sure everyone gets along I gotta be good I gotta be strong I gotta be the best son in the world
CHORUS	In the world
SCOTT	I gotta be good
CHORUS	Try so hard
SCOTT	I gotta be strong
CHORUS	Try so hard
SCOTT	I gotta be the best damn son in the world I gotta be good
CHORUS	Means a lot
SCOTT	I gotta be strong
CHORUS	You gotta be strong
SCOTT	I gotta be the best son in the world And I will find a way To keep our family tight And I will find a way I just gotta
JAKE	Not to worry, Scott, with that A+ the sky's the limit. If you play your cards right, Fiona, you might be lucky too. *(He winks at her.)*
FIONA	What are you talking about?

JAKE	I'm talking about your parents… Since my parents' divorce, they've been trying to be my best friends. If I want something they'll fight over who's going to buy it for me. They fight over who'll have me over on weekends.
FIONA	Yikes!
JAKE	They love me. That's why they're fighting so much. It means I matter to them. It's kind of flattering.
FIONA	Really?
JAKE	Well sort of…
FIONA	So you don't like it.
JAKE	I didn't say that. All I'm saying is that it… It plays a huge part in my life and I manage. I learned that, for me, everything seems to come in twos… and I've accepted that.
FIONA	I hear a piano. Are you gonna sing too?
JAKE	Sure am!

JAKE'S SONG

JAKE	From Mom's to Dad's From Dad's to school From school to Dad's From Dad's to Mom's From Mom's to school From school to soccer practice From soccer practice to violin lessons From violin lessons to the Jetta From the Jetta to Mom's From Mom's to school And that's how my week goes

Jake here has
Two homes
Two beds
Two sets of toothbrushes
Two birthday cakes
Two sets of everything

From Mom's to Dad's cottage
From Dad's cottage to Mom's house
From Mom's house to a summer camp that I don't want to go to
From summer camp, Jake goes back to Mom's
From Mom's to Disneyland with Mom and... Harry
From Disneyland to Dad's and... Nancy's

Jake here has
Two homes
Two beds
Two sets of toothbrushes
Two birthday cakes
Two sets of everything

See, Fiona, it's not that bad.

FIONA   I don't know, Jake. You're running all over the place. How do
           you keep on top of things?

JAKE   Agenda, cellphone, and Blackberry.

FIONA   Wow!

JAKE   Yup! Sky's the limit, Waddington... Sky's the limit!

SCENE 5

*Back at the Waddingtons'. FIONA is lying on the floor watching
television. DANIEL and SUSAN are standing behind her.*

DANIEL   Your mom and I have something important to tell you.

FIONA   Oh yeah? What is it? *(to herself)* Sky's the limit, sky's the limit,
                  sky's the limit.

SUSAN   Life is full of changes.

                  *FIONA has an "all-knowing" smile on her face, she keeps repeat-
                  ing in a low voice "sky's the limit."*

                  We have to adapt to changes sometimes. It can be scary some-
                  times and sometimes it's not that scary. It can be a combina-
                  tion of both too…

                  *SUSAN and DANIEL are talking to FIONA. The audience doesn't
                  hear the entire conversation. FIONA's looks interact with her par-
                  ents' but isn't very engaged by the conversation. FIONA later gets
                  up and exits.*

                  (whispering as an aside to DANIEL) Well that went over well,
                  wouldn't you say?

                  SUSAN and DANIEL exit.

SCENE 6

                  *Next day, after school, FIONA, SCOTT, JAKE, and VALERIE are
                  talking at their lockers.*

SCOTT   Okay, so let me get this straight. Your parents sat down with
                  you and talked your ears off. The big "talk" was about "adjust-
                  ing to changes"?!

FIONA   That's basically it… yup.

JAKE   Hmmm… Interesting. They're trying to soften the blow.
                  They're making sure that you're not gonna blame them for

being messed up 'cause of their split. They might feel a little guilty.

VALERIE   If you ask me, I think her parents wanted to let Ona know about their divorce or separation, got cold feet and chickened out. I heard her parents arguing when I was on the phone with Ona... I heard everything. Her mom said "Fine!" and her dad said "Fine!" back and it was super loud too. So... I think it's safe to say that Ona's parents are going to be separated or divorced. It's just a matter of time. We need to be there for her and support her in any way we can. That's what Dr. Phil said once when he had a family on the show.

JAKE   What was the show about?

VALERIE   I was watching *The Simpsons* and I only caught the last five minutes of the show. I'm pretty sure it was a show about divorce and separation.

SCOTT   But maybe it wasn't. You can't be sure. You just said that you caught the last five minutes of the show.

VALERIE   God! I know what I'm talking about, okay? Ona, I'm just telling you what I saw on *Dr. Phil*. I know a lot about life and stuff thanks to him.

JAKE   Oh brother! I hear a song coming on...

VALERIE   You got that right! I know how to sing. Get a load of this!

JAKE   Uhhh... You don't have to sing. It's okay, if you don't sing we won't hold it against you. It might not be such a bad idea.

VALERIE   Shut up, Jake!

VALERIE'S SONG

VALERIE   They say I'm just a kid, who doesn't know much about life
And I learn from Dr. Phil, who talks to housewives or low-lifes,
trying to find resolution to their strife—

(in a regular speaking voice) "Yes it rhymes!"

And I learned that...
Life is not easy, it can be dreary, it can be lousy, take it from me
Life can be funny, guess that sounds flaky

JAKE   *(to the audience)* Sorry about that, folks.

VALERIE   Shut it!
Back to the song...

But I don't give a shit what you may think

(in a regular speaking voice) "Can I say shit? Who cares, it's my
musical number."

They say that we're just kids and assume that we don't know
what's going on
But this little thirteen-year-old's observations are dead-on.
Dead-on!
I'm Valerie Cooper and I'm in grade eight
My parents have split, I wonder if that's fate
I've got an annoying little brother "Johnny" who keeps
snooping around my stuff
I call him the "Mischief"

(in a regular speaking voice) "I need to find something that
rhymes with stuff. Stuff, mischief, stuff, mischief. Pronounced
"mischuff" so it rhymes."

He seems to take it well
And I'm thinking what the hell?

He acts like nothing happened
While I'm feeling like I'm in a dead end
But you know what?
Life is not easy, it can be dreary, it can be lousy, take it from me
Life can be funny, guess that sounds flaky... So I'll end this
song with simple doo-doo-doo-doo-doo!

JAKE   That was pretty neat. The ending was... well...

VALERIE   Shut up, Jake.

FIONA   I guess it can't hurt to watch a bit of *Dr. Phil.* What time did
you say it was on?

VALERIE   Five p.m., Monday to Friday on channel eight. Right after
Oprah. It's gonna help you cope with things. He's sooo good.
Right, Scott?

SCOTT   I wouldn't watch that stuff if I were you.

VALERIE   You're my boyfriend, Scott. We're supposed to be on the same
page. This is not good. We need to talk.

SCOTT   Can't. We have hockey practice. *(checks the clock)* It's four
already. We better go. I'll call you tonight.

JAKE   Ladies, it's been real. *(He exits.)*

SCOTT   Wait up.

JAKE   *(offstage)* Do your thing. I'll wait for you outside.

> SCOTT *and* VALERIE *are kissing, and it feels like forever while*
> FIONA *looks away.*

SCOTT   Bye. Later, Fiona.

FIONA   Yeah, later, Scott.

VALERIE	*(She sighs.)* I love him. *(in a really serious tone)* I think I'm ready to let him touch my boobs. It'll strengthen the relationship. That's how relationships work.
FIONA	*(She laughs.)* Did you tell him that?
VALERIE	Are you crazy?

They both exit.

SCENE 7

Friday night at the Waddingtons'. FIONA *is in the kitchen and is equipped with a video camera and an iPhone. She turns the camera on and faces it toward her.*

| FIONA | My... Uh... Susan and Daniel Waddington are in the house right now as we speak. Today is when I'm going to confront them about the imminent approach of their divorce or separation—we don't know yet.

But if my Spidey senses are correct *(winks at the camera and mouths "I love you, Tobey Maguire")*, it's gonna happen real soon, unless I do something about it. |
|---|---|

She walks into the living room. SUSAN *and* DANIEL *are sitting on a couch watching* TV. FIONA *turns off the* TV.

DANIEL	We were watching that. It's ten o'clock, you should be in bed. Why are you still up?
FIONA	We got some more important things to deal with right now; more important than the fact that I'm up past my bedtime. *(She presses play on her iPhone and we hear an audience clapping. She points the camera in* SUSAN's *direction.)* Susan, you're awfully quiet. Is there something on your mind?

SUSAN	Did you just call me Susan?!
FIONA	*(She whispers.)* Right now I'm talking to you as an equal. I'll go back to calling you "Mom" when we're off the air, okay?
DANIEL	What's this all about? Why are you filming us? Why is there an audience clapping?
FIONA	*(She sets the camera on a bookcase facing them. She sits beside DANIEL.)* It's okay, Daniel. Try to relax. Pretend the camera and the audio track are not there. I'd like to thank you for taking part in this. It takes a lot of courage.
DANIEL	You didn't ask us—
FIONA	Daniel, you'll get your chance to speak soon enough. Can I continue?

DANIEL *and* SUSAN *look confused.*

	(She whispers.) It's for a project. *(in a normal tone)* I'm here at the Waddington residence. Meet Susan and Daniel Waddington. They've been married for… How long have you guys been married?
SUSAN	*(still conscious that she's being filmed but is playing along)* Is this for school, honey?
FIONA	*(She whispers.)* Mmmmooooommm, we're on the air. *(in a soothing tone)* I'll be the one asking the questions, yeah?
SUSAN	We've been married for sixteen years.
DANIEL	Fiona, it's late, you should be in bed. What's the point of all this?
FIONA	It's important for you to understand that every action has a reaction. When you pull a bull by its horns you better believe

that he's not gonna put up with it. The action of you pulling the horns of that bull will result in the bull reacting to the pull—positive or negative—and it's the same way when you are dealing with human beings. *(She presses play on her iPhone and we hear an audience clapping.)* Let's not kid ourselves. Earlier you asked me what was the point of all this, do you remember that, Daniel?

DANIEL   Yes, what's the point of all this?

FIONA   I'm here to save your marriage. That's my point. *(She presses play on her iPhone and we hear an audience clapping.)*

SUSAN   *(looking at* FIONA *and at the camera, smiling)* Honey, our marriage is fine.

FIONA   Susan, I'd really appreciate it if you could call me Fiona. Not sweetie or honey; just Fiona during this discussion. Now last week I witnessed the aftermath of a dispute between the two of you during a Sunday dinner.

DANIEL   I don't remember that.

FIONA   Well let me refresh your memory. We were sitting at the table eating Susan's famous President's Choice frozen lasagna. It was really quiet at the table. You, Susan, asked Daniel if he could pass you the salt. And you, Daniel, passed the salt just like that. Now what the hell was that all about? That's what I want to know, that's what we all want to know. *(She presses play on her iPhone and we hear an audience clapping.)*

SUSAN   What's the problem? There's no issue here, Fiona.

FIONA   *(She whispers and smiles.)* Thanks for calling me Fiona. *(in a Dr. Phil tone)* The issue here is that I was full, I asked if I could be excused, then I went to my... uhh... office. You two were clearly arguing because when I called my colleague Valerie, she could hear both of you saying "Fine!" and "Fine!" loudly over the phone. That's the issue here. And we're gonna get to the bottom of this—together. We'll be right back. *(FIONA sings the guitar riff of the theme from* Dr. Phil. *She presses play on her iPhone and we hear an audience clapping. She presses "pause" on the camera.)*

FIONA   *(smiling)* How are you guys feeling? Not too nervous, I hope.

SUSAN   Fiona—

FIONA   You can call me sweetie now, we're off the air. Do you need a glass of water? Kleenex? Do you feel like you might cry—'cause that would be very effective. Dad, what about you?

DANIEL   Fiona—

FIONA   It's okay, sweetie is fine, I told you, we're off the air.

DANIEL   "Sweetie," it's passed your bedtime.

FIONA   Tomorrow is Saturday, Dad. I can sleep in.

DANIEL   Fine, but after the taping you have to go to bed. Promise?

FIONA   Deal.

        SUSAN *whispers to* DANIEL.

SUSAN   What on earth are they teaching her at school? Some project.

DANIEL   Beats me.

FIONA   Okay, are you guys ready?

SUSAN   Yes swee… Fiona.

DANIEL   Ready.

> *FIONA turns the camera back on and sits next to* DANIEL. *FIONA sings the guitar riff of the theme from* Dr. Phil. *She presses play on her iPhone and we hear an audience clapping.*

FIONA We're back with Susan and Daniel. Now over the break Susan said that your marriage was "fine," correct?

SUSAN Yes.

FIONA Do you agree, Daniel?

DANIEL Of course I agree.

FIONA I sense a bit of hostility here.

> SUSAN *gives* FIONA *a look of disapproval.*

(She whispers.) It's for the ratings…

SUSAN Fiona, everything is fine.

FIONA *(looking straight at the camera).* There you have it, folks, the Waddingtons are not divorcing or separating.

DANIEL All parents fight sometimes, it's normal, it happens. Just like you get into fights with your friends sometimes… They're still your friends. Sometimes you have disagreements—

FIONA Thanks, Daniel. *(to the camera, in a Dr. Phil tone)* I'm gonna share something with y'all that might come to you as a shock. Daniel and Susan Waddington are my parents. I'm their daughter. I didn't want to inform you of this until the end of the show. Thanks guys, you can leave now.

> SUSAN *and* DANIEL *get up off the couch and look at* FIONA. *FIONA makes a gesture to leave, whispers "Go!"*

Here are my final thoughts. They call me the Last Unicorn. I'm the only one out of my group of friends whose parents are still together. I am glad my parents are still together. I'm happy that I live with both my parents. This is not to say that living in a single-parent home or rotating to stay at one parent's house to the other is a bad thing. It's great. Families come in different sizes. It's still family. That sums it up for this week's episode of *Fiona*. Thank you to Susan and Daniel for being on the show from the Waddington residence, bye for now!

> *FIONA sings the guitar riff of the theme from* Dr. Phil *as we hear an audience clapping. She turns off the camera.*

DANIEL   Okay, it's a quarter past ten, sweetie. Can I call you "sweetie" now?

FIONA   Dddddaaaaadddddd!

SUSAN   What class is this project for? New media?

FIONA   I'm gonna post it on Myspace and YouTube.

DANIEL   Who's going to see this?

FIONA   Relax, Dad. The only people who are going to see this are friends of friends of friends of friends of friends—around the world.

            No biggie.

DANIEL   I don't like this YouTube and Myspace. It's not natural. It's weird.

FIONA   It's how we connect with one another. This is 2009 not 1989. Telegrams don't cut it anymore.

SUSAN   Excuse me?!

FIONA	Kidding! Stop. Kidding! Stop.
DANIEL	Ha! Ha! That's very funny. Susan, maybe this is a good time to tell Miss Fiona about you know what...
FIONA	What is it?
SUSAN	Remember when your father and I talked about changes and how it can be scary and exciting?
FIONA	Yeah, yeah, yeah... About dealing with "changes."
SUSAN	There are going to be some changes in the house.
FIONA	Divorce or separation?
DANIEL	What?
FIONA	Come on, I can take it. Divorce or separation? It's okay. I guess I won't post the show on YouTube and Myspace. It would be considered as defamation, libel, slander, or something. I could get sued.
SUSAN	I'm pregnant. You're going to have a new brother or sister.
	Silence.
FIONA	What?! No way! Why didn't you tell me before? You guys are still having sex?! Ewww grooooosssssssss! I was so sure you guys were splitting up because of that fight you guys had on Sunday and Valerie, Jake, and Scott convinced me that it was the end for us as a family. Your talk about "changes" and *Dr. Phil*—
SUSAN	Whoa, slow down there. About that argument on Sunday... My heart was set on having a salad as part of our Sunday dinner. Your father forgot to buy the lettuce and I was upset because he promised me he'd buy the lettuce—

DANIEL	But I did buy some the next day.
SUSAN	True.
FIONA	Oh I see. *(SUSAN and DANIEL freeze. To the audience.)* This is the part where I tell you that it was just a big misunderstanding 'cause I thought my parents were gonna split up but in fact they're not splitting up, they're actually having a baby! A baby! I'm gonna be a big sister! So cool! My parents are still having sex—together! Ewwwwww! So gross! *(She regains her composure.)* So bear with me, okay, as I try to put an end to this big mess. *(SUSAN and DANIEL unfreeze. FIONA is talking to her parents.)* You mean to tell me that you guys fought over lettuce?! All this time I thought you guys were splitting up. I posted on my blog about you guys possibly splitting up. I got feedback from people in Iceland, from Burkina Faso, Egypt, giving me advice on how to cope with the situation. I watched *Dr. Phil.*
DANIEL	Well you can post on your blog that everything was blown out of proportion. Please stop watching *Dr. Phil.*
FIONA	It was just a misunderstanding. What a mess I created!
SUSAN	A big mess.
DANIEL	A huge mess!

> DANIEL, SUSAN, *and* FIONA *are laughing like they do after some cheesy* TV *episode from the '70s and '80s.* DANIEL *and* SUSAN *freeze.*

| FIONA | *(to the audience)* Still not satisfied? You're not buying it, are you? Okay then… |

> DANIEL *and* SUSAN *unfreeze.*

| DANIEL | Please stop watching *Dr. Phil.* It's not the way to go about things. |

SUSAN	But you can watch *Oprah* if you want. We've got nothing against *Oprah*.
DANIEL	We love *Oprah*!
FIONA	Deal.
DANIEL	Now you really have to go to bed. I'm serious.
FIONA	Okay. Good night Mom, *(She kisses her on the cheek.)* good night Dad. *(She kisses him on the cheek.)* I'm gonna be a big sister!

She exits singing "I'm gonna be good, I'm gonna be strong. I'm gonna be the best sister in the world! Whoa!"

DANIEL	She thought we were splitting up.
SUSAN	*(laughing in disbelief)* Unreal. It explains why she's been acting so strange lately.
DANIEL	Splitting up?! She actually thought we were splitting up. Kids and their wild imaginations...

They exit.

SCENE 8

It's Monday at noon in the school cafeteria. FIONA and her friends are eating their lunch at their usual table. FIONA is in a very good mood.

SCOTT	Saw your show on YouTube... Cool.
JAKE	Yeah I saw that. I didn't know you hated being called the Last Unicorn. I thought it was kind of cool. I'm sorry.

FIONA	I don't like being called Waddington, Ona, or Fifi for that matter.
VALERIE	I guess I was wrong about your parents splitting up. I'm sorry for cutting your name short too. I thought it sounded cool. You know, like A-Rod, K-Stew, R-Patz—
FIONA	Well I don't like it.
VALERIE	Fine, sorry.
FIONA	I don't want you guys to put stuff in my head. I just went through the worst week of my life. From now on I'll be forming my own opinions on stuff. No more free advice unless I ask you, okay?
JAKE	That's cool.
SCOTT	Okay.
VALERIE	Sure thing, Fiona.
FIONA	Thanks for calling me Fiona, Valerie.
	There is a long silence. Everyone is looking at each other waiting to see who will speak first.
	There's no way around it, guys. We just have to. We have to finish what we started.
SCOTT	Okay.
JAKE	I'm in.
VALERIE	Me too!
JAKE	You can sit that one out if you want. No pressure.

VALERIE   Shut it!!

FIONA   *(to the audience)* This is it, the grand finale!

"ENTIRELY FOR YOU"

CHORUS   Entirely for you
             So you have seen that there's more there to us
             We have shown
             Entirely for you
             So you have seen that there's more there to us
             We have shown

             Valerie
             Cooper
             She can't sing, only thirteen, thinks she's all grown up now
             Scott
             Mason
             World's best son, feels like the world is resting on his shoul-
             ders now
             Jake
             Belvedere
             Latchkey kid, always the clown, way deep inside we know he's
             hurting now
             Fiona
             Waddington
             Future big sis, needs to stand her ground now

             Entirely for you
             So you have seen that there's more there to us
             We have shown
             Entirely for you
             So you have seen that there's more there to us
             We have shown

                 Lights fade a bit.

JAKE	Jake, you're gonna be late for your violin lessons. Don't forget that we're having dinner with Harry tonight. I bought you those Eckos you wanted. Just don't tell your dad about it. I love you.
SCOTT	Kick ass tonight, son. We'll be cheering for you. Make sure you score a goal for me. You got an A- on your history test? That's great! I knew you could do it! I'm so proud of you. Try to get an A on your next one. "Atta boy!"
VALERIE	You need to pick up your brother after school. I'm working late and your dad says that he's got a meeting at three. Probably going out with that Cheryl... Liar! Thanks Val.
FIONA	Meet your new sister, Fiona. Isn't she precious? You're going to make a fine big sister.

A school bell rings.

Blackout.

BEHIND THE SCENES
WITH EDWIGE JEAN-PIERRE

Edwige Jean-Pierre is a bilingual French and English actor, playwright, and librettist with a dynamic sense of humour. Jean-Pierre's adult plays include *Our Lady of Spills* and *Saint Bitch*.

Behind the biographical headlines, Edwige's favourite credits include *Even Darkness is Made of Light* (Rhubarb Festival, AfriCanadian Playwrights' Festival), *Late* (Obsidian Theatre), *If We Were Birds* (Groundswell/SummerWorks), and *Our Lady of Spills* (Theatre Archipelago/Meow Films).

Jean-Pierre's visual arts inspiration for *The Big Mess* was found among Obsidan Theatre Director Philip Akin's amazing art collection during a visit with other members of the Playwrights Unit. "I was looking at this painting of this young girl who is just staring out into space. She looked perturbed and/or preoccupied in her thoughts. What is bugging her? That's what I kept asking myself. I imagined her listening to her parents fighting. That's where the trigger came from."

On the art of playwriting, which is both so mechanical and so creative, the best thing—the fun—for Jean-Pierre is letting her imagination run free. The worst thing about writing plays, and what she says are the most painful times, is when she is dealing with writer's block.

Edwige's next goal is to collaborate on a play with a friend, although that collaborative idea is still in the embryonic stage.

Asked to reflect on Obsidian's contributions to her development, Edwige talked about encouragement. She was allowed to take a risk, to create a piece of musical theatre for young audiences while a member of the Playwrights Unit.

Leaving us with a final impish thought, Edwige Jean-Pierre observed, "My sense of humour is dry, quirky, and absurd and I use it quite a lot when writing plays."

DAUGHTER'S LAST SUPPER
BY REBECCA FISSEHA

CHARACTERS

Daughter: A young woman in her early twenties.

Ghost: A transparent replica of Daughter.

Father: A professional man in his fifties.

Mother: A professional woman in her forties.

Son: A young man in his late twenties.

SETTING

A dining room.

INSPIRATIONS

The painting, of course, and

"...time... stumbled and had accidents and could therefore splinter and
leave an eternalized fragment in a room."
—Gabriel García Márquez, *One Hundred Years of Solitude*

In the dining room, DAUGHTER *sits at an opulent dining table set for four, complete with food and drinks, and lit by a lone ceiling light. The arrangement is ambiguous enough so that it could be breakfast or dinner, half-eaten or half-served. It is very dark outside. Stairs lead to the upper level of the house.*

DAUGHTER *stares at an envelope she holds in her hand.*

In the distance, a church bell tolls. With each toll of the bell, the darkness outside fades a little. On the fifth toll of the bell, there is a hint of dawn.

DAUGHTER *finally gathers up her courage to open the envelope. She takes out a letter. From the way she reads the letter, it is clear that she herself wrote it—she reads it to confirm what she already knows.*

The sound of footsteps comes from the stairs. DAUGHTER *quickly puts the letter back in the envelope and slides it into a folded newspaper on the table.*

GHOST *enters and sits at the table.*

GHOST   Can I have it now?

DAUGHTER   What?

GHOST   The newspaper.

DAUGHTER   No!

GHOST	You're still not done with it?
DAUGHTER	No, no I'm not.
GHOST	You're unbelievable. What happened to you?
DAUGHTER	What do you mean what happened to me?
GHOST	You're not the same anymore.
DAUGHTER	I'm exactly as I've always been.
GHOST	You don't treat me like you used to.
DAUGHTER	Yes I do.
GHOST	You don't love me anymore.
DAUGHTER	Of course I do.
GHOST	You don't need me like I need you. You see!
DAUGHTER	See what?
GHOST	This! We're fighting.
DAUGHTER	People fight.
GHOST	People. We never used to fight.
DAUGHTER	Things are different now.
GHOST	I know, that's what I've been saying.
DAUGHTER	I mean things have to start changing.
GHOST	Since when?

DAUGHTER	Because I need to get away.
GHOST	You do? To where?
DAUGHTER	Just away, out of here. I don't mean forever, I'll come back to visit.
GHOST	And what am I supposed to do in the meantime?
DAUGHTER	I don't know.
GHOST	Tell them about me.
DAUGHTER	No!
GHOST	Why not?
DAUGHTER	Because they wouldn't understand.
GHOST	You can't leave me behind.
DAUGHTER	Why?
GHOST	All by myself, I'll die!
DAUGHTER	You are dead! And I will be too, if I spend another day in here. It's time we went our separate ways.
GHOST	When is that?
DAUGHTER	When they get the letter.
GHOST	Oh right, the letter you've been writing forever.
DAUGHTER	I wrote it this time.
GHOST	Sure.

DAUGHTER   You'll see.

GHOST   You did?

DAUGHTER   It's the only way out, why wouldn't I write it?

GHOST   What about me?

DAUGHTER   What about you?

GHOST   I'll die!

DAUGHTER   Get up and leave.

GHOST   You know I can't.

DAUGHTER   Yes you can.

GHOST   Will you tell them about me?

DAUGHTER   No.

GHOST   I can't leave if you don't tell them about me.

DAUGHTER   I know. Fine.

GHOST   Fine? You'll tell them, really?

DAUGHTER   Yes.

GHOST   Okay! You really did write it, didn't you?

DAUGHTER   Just one question. What am I supposed to say?

GHOST   To them?

DAUGHTER   Yes to them… what am I supposed to say to them? I've already used up everything in the letter. So give me something.

GHOST	Uh…
DAUGHTER	What am I supposed to say… oh there's this other girl just like me and she's been sitting at the table with us for seventeen years, she's a ghost. So while I'm gone can you please be nice to her and talk to her so she doesn't get lonely. This is the first time that she will be without me, so she will be very sad. Make sure to talk to her.
GHOST	Why are you making it out like it's just me who is going to be lonely?
DAUGHTER	Is that what I'm supposed to say?
GHOST	No.
DAUGHTER	What is it then? Huh, what is it?
GHOST	You know.
DAUGHTER	No, I don't know. Do tell me.
GHOST	Yes you do.

In the distance, a church bell tolls.

DAUGHTER	Here we go again. No I don't.
GHOST	Yes you do.

The bell tolls.

DAUGHTER	No I don't.
GHOST	Yes you do.

The bell tolls.

DAUGHTER	No I don't.
GHOST	Yes you do.

The bell tolls.

DAUGHTER	No I don't.
GHOST	Yes you do.

The bell tolls.

DAUGHTER	No I don't.
GHOST	Yes you do.

The bell tolls a sixth time. A little daylight creeps in.

DAUGHTER	They'll start coming down in an hour.
GHOST	So what?
DAUGHTER	So I should leave the table.
GHOST	Easy for you to say.
DAUGHTER	You want them to find me still sitting at the dinner table?
GHOST	Maybe that's what we need.
DAUGHTER	What?
GHOST	For them to wonder why you're still here.
DAUGHTER	And then what?
GHOST	You can explain that I was nagging you and wouldn't let you leave.

DAUGHTER	You.
GHOST	Yeah.

DAUGHTER considers this.

That's a good way to ease into it.

DAUGHTER	It won't work.
GHOST	That's impossible.
DAUGHTER	Have you been living with this family for seventeen years or haven't you?
GHOST	Yeah, but when did you ever spend the whole night at the table?
DAUGHTER	Believe me. I could be dancing on the table and they'll still carry on like it's just another day.
GHOST	They ignore you too?
DAUGHTER	Now you see why I have to leave.

The bell tolls seven times. More daylight creeps into the room.

Any minute now.

Seven steps sound down the stairs.

FATHER comes in dressed for work and sits at the table. He unfolds the newspaper that is beside DAUGHTER and holds it out in front of him.

FATHER	*(reads)* "Australian sells own life."
DAUGHTER	How did he do that?

FATHER   *(reads)* "…successful applicant bid… five thousand seven hundred and ninety American dollars… to become Bruce, Nicael Bruce… right down to spending Thanksgiving with his parents… inheriting… an ex from a painful breakup."

> FATHER *laughs, reads silently, then starts to read aloud again, pausing to chuckle or laugh in between segments.*

(reads) "Aged twenty-six… says he's not sure why he did it… sold his name, phone number, and all his possessions… a surfboard, a laptop, a wonky pushbike, photos, and a 'nice lamp'… on the Internet auction site… philosophy student… unable to explain why he sold his life…"

> FATHER *continues to read silently.*

GHOST   I can't believe it!

DAUGHTER   I know, the things people will do for attention.

GHOST   He hasn't said anything.

DAUGHTER   Oh he always speaks newspaperese… why am I having to explain this to you?

GHOST   I mean… I mean!

DAUGHTER   I told you. I said it wouldn't make a difference.

GHOST   Well you didn't even try.

DAUGHTER   Try what?

GHOST   You didn't even try to tell him.

DAUGHTER   Well if he didn't mention that I've sat here all night, how am I supposed to tell him about you?

GHOST   What does one have to do with another?

DAUGHTER   I don't know, you started it.

GHOST   I started it? I started it by asking you to tell them. I didn't say you should wait for them to notice you.

DAUGHTER   Yes you did.

GHOST   No I didn't.

DAUGHTER   Yes. You did.

GHOST   Okay fine, now I changed my mind. Just tell him.

DAUGHTER   Fine.

GHOST   Fine.

                    FATHER laughs and reads aloud, chuckling in between segments.

FATHER   "Motivating factors... boredom... intrigue as to what constitutes a life... what made him who he was... hoping to make a point that the amount and type of things that are for sale in this world are insane and wasteful... the wining bidder would take a four-week training course in how to be Nicael... including lessons on how to surf, climb, skateboard, fire twirl, and do handstands... two months of on-call support afterward... be introduced to all Bruce's friends and potential lovers..."

                    FATHER resumes reading silently.

DAUGHTER   *(to GHOST)* How's this... meet this other girl who is just like me, she's been sitting at the table with us for seventeen years, she's a ghost. So while I'm gone can you please be nice to her and talk to her so she doesn't get lonely? This is the first time that she will be without me so she will be very sad. Make sure to talk to her, even if you can't see her because she's a ghost. Trust me, she's there.

GHOST   Well you don't have to say she's a ghost.

DAUGHTER   What are you?

GHOST   I'm not a ghost.

DAUGHTER   Oh?

GHOST   You know who I am.

DAUGHTER   No I don't.

GHOST   Yes you do.

In the distance, the church bell tolls.

DAUGHTER   No I don't.

GHOST   Yes you do.

The bell tolls.

DAUGHTER   No I don't.

GHOST   Yes you do.

The bell tolls.

DAUGHTER   No I don't.

GHOST   Yes you do.

The bell tolls.

DAUGHTER   No I don't.

GHOST   Yes you do.

            The bell tolls.

DAUGHTER   No I don't.

GHOST   Yes you do.

            The bell tolls.

DAUGHTER   No I don't.

GHOST   Yes you ·do.

            The bell tolls.

DAUGHTER   No I don't.

GHOST   Yes you do.

            The bell tolls an eighth time.

            *By now morning has flooded into the room. Eight steps
            sound down the stairs.* MOTHER *comes in, also dressed for
            work.*

            Throughout the conversation between MOTHER *and* DAUGHTER,
            FATHER *can be heard softly rereading the entire article about the
            Australian.*

MOTHER   Oatmeal is finished?

FATHER   Australian sells own life on the Internet.

DAUGHTER   I didn't sleep.

MOTHER   Must be finished.

DAUGHTER	I'm not sick or anything. I'm pretty sure I'm not sick. My room is too cold though.
MOTHER	There's not even any coffee.
DAUGHTER	I couldn't eat dinner either.
MOTHER	And where's the juice?
DAUGHTER	I'm so worried about the letter from the university.
MOTHER	We'll just do bread and jam for this morning.
DAUGHTER	It should have been here a week ago.
MOTHER	But I thought I bought extra oatmeal and put some in the top cabinet.
DAUGHTER	Could that mean I can't go anywhere?
GHOST	I hope not.
DAUGHTER	You're so evil.
GHOST	I'm evil?
DAUGHTER	Yeah, how could you say that?
GHOST	'Cause then you wouldn't be going.
DAUGHTER	Stop thinking about only yourself for a change.
GHOST	Who else am I supposed to think about?
MOTHER	No oatmeal, no coffee, no juice. We're going to be late.
DAUGHTER	Me.

GHOST	That's what I'm trying to do.
DAUGHTER	No one asked you to.
MOTHER	The mail is not even in yet.
GHOST	Great progress you're making with this.
MOTHER	*(to FATHER)* That girl is not eating. She is not sleeping.
DAUGHTER	*(to GHOST)* Shut up. I think she heard me.
GHOST	Of course she hears you.
DAUGHTER	No she doesn't.
GHOST	How couldn't she, you're right there.
DAUGHTER	Didn't you just see?
GHOST	I'm starting to wonder who's the ghost here.
DAUGHTER	Oh so you *are* a ghost now.
GHOST	I've always been.
DAUGHTER	Right. When things aren't going well you decide to be the ghost and let me take the blame.
GHOST	Is that why you're running away?
DAUGHTER	I'm not running away. I have a perfect right to leave.

FATHER reads aloud to both MOTHER and DAUGHTER.

FATHER	"'Lifestyle is very social. It includes a lot of going out,' Nicael noted in his eBay advert... 'Friends will treat you exactly as

they have treated me. All of these features will be transferred over to the winning applicant.'"

MOTHER   Coffee, at least coffee.

> *MOTHER leaves the dining room. FATHER continues to read aloud.*

FATHER   *(reads)* "…legal identity, passport, qualifications, and future inheritance were not for sale… on the nicael.com website, Nicael writes he would like to make a contribution to those who have nothing by donating to a charity… raised only a modest one hundred dollars…"

> *FATHER reads silently for a bit and then flips the newspaper page, chuckling to himself in amazement. MOTHER calls from the kitchen.*

MOTHER   The juice is finished too.

GHOST   Nicael. What kind of a stupid name is that?

DAUGHTER   At least he's got one.

GHOST   I think they meant to name him "Michael" but half of the "M" got erased off or something. I just wonder which half.

DAUGHTER   What do you mean which half?

GHOST   Was it the first half of the "M" or the last half of the "M" that got erased off?

DAUGHTER   Either way it makes an "N," doesn't it? And who told you it was erased off?

GHOST   True, it could have been chopped off. Or the ink could have run out.

DAUGHTER	Then that would make it the last half of the "M" that was never written.
GHOST	Or the first, if the pen was just a little dry at first.
DAUGHTER	Oh for God's sake, what are we doing?
GHOST	I get it! The dude is maintaining that he still has a part of himself, even after selling himself on the Net, so by keeping half the "M" …
DAUGHTER	Okay genius, you got it.
GHOST	Don't be so negative.
DAUGHTER	Well I'm irritated. You won't shut up. I can't leave because the letter still hasn't arrived yet.
GHOST	You didn't even write it, did you?
DAUGHTER	Of course I did!
GHOST	Then what happened?
DAUGHTER	It must have gotten lost in the mail.
GHOST	You're free to go, letter or no letter.
DAUGHTER	Uh, no I'm not.
GHOST	No, really, I'll be fine. Go ahead.
DAUGHTER	No, you won't be fine.
GHOST	Yes I will.
DAUGHTER	No you won't.

SON comes in dressed in casual day clothes like DAUGHTER *and heads for the front door on the other side of the room.* FATHER *returns to the page he was first reading on the newspaper.*

FATHER   *(reads)* "...sells own life on the Internet... eBay..." *(to* SON*)* eBay?

SON stops.

SON   It's an Internet site where people buy and sell stuff. Like an online store.

SON starts to head for door.

FATHER   *(reads)* "...a surfboard, a laptop, a wonky pushbike..." *(to* SON*)* Wonky pushbike?

SON stops.

SON   I don't know.

FATHER   *(to* SON*)* Wonky pushbike.

SON   I don't know.

SON starts to head for the door again.

FATHER   *(reads)* "...wonky... pushbike... ridderstrade... eBay auction winner is known only as ridderstrade..." *(to* SON*)* Ridderstrade?

SON stops.

SON   Like it says, the eBay auction winner, that's his name.

FATHER   "Ridderstrade"?

SON   That's his name.

SON begins to move again.

FATHER   *(reads)* "…including lessons on how to surf, climb, skateboard, fire twirl…" *(to SON)* Fire twirl?

SON   I don't—

FATHER   *(reads)* "Skateboard, fire twirl, and do handstands…" *(to SON)* Handsta—?

SON   It's a kind of acrob—

FATHER   *(reads)* "As well as two months of on-call support afterward…" Australian sells own life on Internet!

SON finally makes his exit.

DAUGHTER   I'm about to lose it!

GHOST   Really, go ahead. I'll be fine.

DAUGHTER   You're not going to survive without me.

GHOST   Yes I will.

DAUGHTER   No you won't.

The bell tolls.

GHOST   Yes I will.

DAUGHTER   No you won't.

The bell tolls.

GHOST   Yes I will.

DAUGHTER   No you won't.

The bell tolls.

GHOST   Yes I will.

DAUGHTER   No you won't.

The bell tolls.

GHOST   Yes I will.

DAUGHTER   No you won't.

The bell tolls.

GHOST   Yes I will.

DAUGHTER   No you won't.

The bell tolls.

GHOST   Yes I will.

DAUGHTER   No you won't.

The bell tolls.

GHOST   Yes I will.

DAUGHTER   No you won't.

The bell tolls.

GHOST   Yes I will.

DAUGHTER   No you won't.

The bell tolls a ninth time.

FATHER   Own life!

> *FATHER chuckles a final chuckle, folds up the newspaper, and leaves it on the table as he found it. MOTHER comes in and they exit together. SON returns.*

SON   *(to DAUGHTER)* Where's the mail?

GHOST   I don't know.

SON   *(to GHOST)* I wasn't asking you.

DAUGHTER   There wasn't any today.

SON   There's always mail.

GHOST   Today there wasn't.

SON   Shut up.

DAUGHTER   Maybe it was all junk mail.

SON   The day you write that letter is the day you die.

> *SON exits. DAUGHTER picks up the newspaper and starts leafing through it.*

GHOST   So no letter today either.

DAUGHTER   Nope.

GHOST   So we continue to wait.

DAUGHTER   Yep.

GHOST   Where are you going to go, when it comes?

DAUGHTER   Just pretend I'm in the next room whenever you're feeling lonely.

GHOST   How well did that work the first time you tried it? Isn't that why we've been in this mess since?

DAUGHTER   Well somebody had to do the dirty work. I was trying to protect you.

GHOST   Thanks for the effort but I'd like to reverse time and get my life back.

DAUGHTER   Just as soon as Nicael returns the seven grand to ridderstrade.

GHOST   Maybe in tomorrow's paper they'll say he did.

DAUGHTER   Maybe. So we wait for tomorrow's paper.

GHOST   Fine. Can I have that when you're finished?

DAUGHTER   By then it will already be tomorrow.

              DAUGHTER continues to idly leaf through the newspaper. GHOST fumes silently.

              In the distance, the bell tolls seven times in reverse. With each reversed toll, daylight recedes from the room, swallowing GHOST with it. At the final toll, all is dark again save for the ceiling light. DAUGHTER is alone at the table, leafing forward through the newspaper pages. FATHER comes in. He and all the other family members that come in are all in their pyjamas.

FATHER   Where are the others?

DAUGHTER   They're coming.

FATHER   What are we having today? *(He scans the table.)* Where's the wine?

              MOTHER comes in.

MOTHER   Oh, the wine, I'll go get it.

> *MOTHER goes out to get the wine. FATHER seats himself at the head of the table.*

FATHER   Did you read that piece about—

DAUGHTER   The Australian? Yes.

FATHER   Amazing, isn't it?

DAUGHTER   It's repeated from yesterday.

FATHER   Eat, eat.

> *DAUGHTER folds up the newspaper and starts to help herself to the food. MOTHER comes in with the wine.*

MOTHER   Here it is.

FATHER   Ah, excellent.

MOTHER   Should I open it?

FATHER   Where's your brother?

DAUGHTER   I'll go get him.

> *DAUGHTER leaves the table and goes upstairs. Shortly after, muffled sounds of argument between her and SON come from upstairs. They stomp down the stairs and enter the dining room. DAUGHTER is shaking and holding a crumpled envelope. She sits at her chair and diligently smoothes out the envelope as she speaks. All members of the family are now seated and eating.*

I found him when he was about to tear this open. How could you do that? You don't even know what's in it!

FATHER   What is it?

DAUGHTER   It's not even addressed to you.

MOTHER   *(handing* SON *the wine bottle)* Here, open this.

SON   It's addressed to the family name, I thought it was junk mail.

                He takes the bottle from MOTHER *and opens it.*

FATHER   *(to* DAUGHTER*)* Open it then.

DAUGHTER   I'll open it when he is gone.

                SON *opens the wine and passes it to* DAUGHTER, *who snatches
                it from him. She pours herself some and returns it to* FATHER.
                He pours himself a glass of wine and passes it back to MOTHER.

FATHER   Ahhhh! Excellent.

SON   It's Cabernet—

FATHER   Oh, Cabernet Sauvignon!

SON   No, Cabernet Fr—

FATHER   Not Cabernet Sauvi—?

SON   No, Cabernet Franc.

FATHER   Yes, French wine, Cabernet Sauvignon.

SON   Yes it's French but it's also Cabernet Franc.

FATHER   From France.

DAUGHTER   It's a French wine called Cabernet that comes as Cabernet
                Sauvignon or as Cabernet Franc! Jesus!

FATHER	Ah! What's the Franc?
SON	I don't know?
FATHER	Cabernet Franc?

SON shrugs.

DAUGHTER	Obviously, it's a type of Cabernet.
MOTHER	Open the letter, dear.
DAUGHTER	No, I want to be alone when I open it.

The church bell tolls eight times, during which members of the family finish eating and leave the table in the order of FATHER, SON, MOTHER.

Alone, DAUGHTER contemplates the envelope.

In the distance, a church bell tolls. With each toll of the bell, the darkness outside fades a little. On the fifth toll of the bell, there is a hint of dawn.

DAUGHTER finally gathers up her courage to open the envelope. She takes out a letter. From the way she reads the letter, it is clear that she herself wrote it—she reads it to confirm what she already knows.

The sound of footsteps comes from the stairs. DAUGHTER quickly puts the letter back in the envelope and slides it into a folded newspaper on the table.

GHOST enters and sits at the table.

GHOST	Can I have it now?
DAUGHTER	What?

GHOST   The paper.

DAUGHTER   No!

GHOST   You're still not done with it?

DAUGHTER   No, no I'm not.

GHOST   You're unbelievable.

DAUGHTER   Whatever.

GHOST   What happened to you?

DAUGHTER   What do you mean what happened to me?

GHOST   You're not the same anymore.

DAUGHTER   I'm exactly as I've always been.

The bell tolls.

Blackout.

The end.

Behind the Scenes
With Rebecca Fisseha

Rebecca Fisseha has a B.A. in theatre from York university and an M.A. in communication and culture from Ryerson and York Universities. Her plays have been produced by b current performing arts and at the SummerWorks Theatre Festival.

Fisseha's three favourite credits/gigs are eclectic. As a writer she has loved creating and witnessing the production of *Wise Woman* while she was artist-in-residence at the b current festival. Her favourite role as an actor was Anowa in the title role of the drama based in Ghana. Finally, she is a visual artist with memorable T-shirt artwork created for the rock.paper.sistahz festival.

In preparation for her contribution to the *Mussorgsky Project*, Rebecca spent time with the artwork in the home of Philip Akin. "The inspiration came from a painting of two women at a kitchen table. At the time, I was also reading *One Hundred Years of Solitude* by Gabriel García Márquez. The mood of the painting and tone of the novel blended to produce what has become *Daughter's Last Supper*."

The best thing about writing plays, says Fisseha, is the "knowledge that what currently only exists as words on a page will one day become a live experience, as opposed to film, for example, where the product is distanced from the audience many times over."

For Rebecca the creative possibility of live performance is also the worst thing about writing plays. She observes that "whatever she writes has to be feasible within the constraints of a stage, while at the same time giving herself the freedom to write in whatever way she feels compelled to, and trusting that the challenges of staging can be met by the future director." In spite of this, she believes playwrights must always bear in mind the limitations of live theatre.

Looking down the road to future projects, Rebecca has many in mind. She would like to see *Wise Woman* published, do the second draft of her next play *Drama* (or turn it into a novel), complete her screenwriting program, and begin a career as a film and television writer. Obsidian Theatre Company has contributed greatly to Fisseha's development. She is delighted to be published for the first time as a result of having participated in the Playwrights Unit.

How Do I Forgive My Dying Father? (Abridged Version)
by Laurence Anthony

voice give just granite company black theatre
OBSIDIAN ENCOURAGEMENT GLASS STRONG JET
SPACE voice give just granite COMPANY BLACK
THEATRE OBSIDIAN ENCOURAGEMENT GLASS
HARD STRONG SPACE JET voice give JUST
GRANITE COMPANY BLACK THEATRE
OBSIDIAN ENCOURAGEMENT GLASS SPAC

CHARACTERS

Will

Maya

Christine

Jack

Shelley

François

Noah—offstage

Alison—offstage

ACT I

Early morning. Five a.m. We're in an exposed-brick loft. A couch is up against the wall of a living room. WILL, a thirty-one-year-old writer, is half-asleep on the couch, tossing and turning. His sister, MAYA, a recently returned soldier, has been staying in his bedroom until she buys her own place. A cellphone rings in WILL's room. Rings again. Again.

MAYA, twenty-eight, a soldier, toned and fit, emerges from the room where we heard the cellphone ringing.

MAYA   *(whispering)* Will. Will, get up.

WILL   *(mumbling)* For what?

MAYA   Will, just get up.

WILL looks at the alarm clock. Too early for him to be up; today or any day. He holds up the clock so MAYA can see. He places it back down on the table. That should do the trick he thinks.

Will, I'm not playing with you right now. Get out of bed.

WILL turns over on the couch, his back facing MAYA. MAYA pulls the comforter off of him. He doesn't budge. She walks to the bathroom, we hear water running and she returns with a cup of cold water. She throws it on WILL. He jumps up. It's freezing.

WILL	Dammit, Maya, what the hell is wrong with you? This isn't the army, okay? You're back home now. *(a beat)* Damn, girl. What is it now?
MAYA	It's Dad.

> WILL *throws a sweater on, walks to the kitchen and begins smoking.*

WILL	You eating breakfast?
MAYA	Not right now. Didn't you just hear me?
WILL	I just heard you, you said you don't want any breakfast.
MAYA	You know I'm not talking about the breakfast, Will.
WILL	Then I have no idea what you're talking about.
MAYA	I'm talking about Dad.
WILL	What about him?
MAYA	He's in the hospital. He's been there for a few days.

> WILL *takes a drag from his cigarette.*

WILL	How does this relate to me?
MAYA	Because he's your father, Will, and he's sick.
WILL	Well, wuppty friggin do, hallelujah, and praise Jesus! I don't care. You shouldn't care either.
MAYA	You know…
WILL	And he's not my father.
MAYA	I would've thought you'd be over it.

WILL	*(calm)* Well, you should know better than that, sis.
	He reaches for a pack of oats.
	You want some?
MAYA	No, thank you. You should really quit smoking, you know.
WILL	I know.
MAYA	He's dying of cancer.
WILL	I'm not him.
MAYA	Mom would've hated it.
	WILL looks at her. A beat.
WILL	I know. She would've.
	He starts making the oats.
MAYA	He's really sick this time.
WILL	*(sympathetic)* How sick?
MAYA	Worse than before. They don't think he's got much longer.
WILL	*(unsympathetic)* That's too bad.
MAYA	You're a class act, bro.
	Will, I'm heading there later today. I'd like you to come with me.
WILL	And hey, I'd like to play for the Lakers, but guess what?
MAYA	I'm beginning to see why Alison left you alone.

She closes the door. WILL *sits in silence for a beat.*

WILL   Oh sure! Throw the Alison card out there! That'll win me over.

            WILL*'s cellphone is ringing.*

            (over the phone) Alison, stop yelling. Alison, I can't talk to you when you're like this... How are you gonna ask me that...? That's not even a question! Of course I wanna see Noah. He's my son... I'm trying, I am. It's all this... Alison? Don't hang up! Dammit!

            He stands, defeated. He pops the collar on his peacoat and exits.

            End of Act I

ACT II

We hear the sound of an EKG *beeping. It continues to beep as we're introduced to* JACK *and his wife,* SHELLEY. JACK *is lying in his hospital bed, he's clearly dying and sick. Traces of his former build barely remain. He was once athletic.* SHELLEY *is a diminutive woman in her fifties, but very attractive, and we can see she's led the privileged life as a judge's wife. She looks expensive, but not tacky.*

SHELLEY   Samantha and her husband said they'd come tomorrow. Their dog died, so the kids are really upset.

JACK   I'll probably be seeing the dog soon.

SHELLEY   Jack, please! Why would you say that?

JACK   Sorry, sweetheart, a bit of morbid humour.

SHELLEY   Well, it's not funny, baby. I don't know how you can be so cavalier right now. But I suppose that's why I love you.

JACK	I thought it was because of my great looks and sexual prowess.
SHELLEY	There hasn't been much of that lately, sweetie.
JACK	Hmm. Touché, my dear. But you know if I wasn't here, I'd be tearing that right up!
SHELLEY	*(laughs)* I know. You're crazy, but I know.
JACK	What about our kids? Have you spoken to François?
SHELLEY	Yeah, his flight is coming in tonight. He'll be here tomorrow as well.
JACK	Whoa! Let's put up the balloons. Tomorrow's looking like a party.
SHELLEY	I didn't call Jessica, like you asked. But I think we should.
JACK	For what? She's halfway across the world. Just make sure you send her that letter when… well, you know when.
SHELLEY	That's not happening for a long time, baby.
JACK	You know better than that.

      Silence.

SHELLEY	It was nice to see Maya earlier. She looks so grown-up. Miss Soldier in the army. She's something. I know how proud you are.
JACK	I am. She's amazing. These past few years talking with her, spending time with her… it's been great. A lieutenant now. My little girl! Imagine that.
SHELLEY	She's a strong woman. Just like her father.
JACK	No. Like her mother was.

The EKG *beeps continue.*

What about Will?

SHELLEY   I don't know, honey.

JACK   I do.

SHELLEY   No, you don't know either. He may come. He may change his mind.

> *The lights fade out.*

> *They fade back on. We're in another flashback.* WILL's *mother,* CHRISTINE, *stands in a room. She cleans as grown-up* WILL *sits down playing with his toys.*

WILL   Mommy, look!

CHRISTINE   Wow! That's amazing, Will. Did you finish reading your book though?

WILL   Yes, Mommy. I read the entire book.

CHRISTINE   Good. I'm proud of you. Dinner will be ready soon, so finish playing with your toys.

WILL   Okay, Mommy. Can I have five more minutes?

CHRISTINE   Five minutes and that's it.

WILL   YES!

> *The apartment door opens and slams shut.* JACK *enters the room.*

JACK   *(yelling)* What the hell is going on?

CHRISTINE   Jack, what are you talking about?

WILL is playing with his toys. CHRISTINE stops cleaning and is looking at JACK.

JACK

I'm playing ball today and I have to hear about you dancing with some guy at a club?

CHRISTINE

What? Are you crazy?

JACK

No, I'm not crazy, Christine! Ronnie told me he saw you and all your little tramp friends at a club.

CHRISTINE

First of all, watch your language around me and Will. Second of all, we were there for Mariah's birthday.

JACK is moving closer to CHRISTINE. WILL stops playing with his toys. He's watching this unfold in front of him.

JACK

And that's why you have to dance with some guy and embarrass me.

CHRISTINE

You need to stop listening to your ignorant friends who don't know what is going on. And don't come in here raising your voice to me in front of my son.

JACK is in front of her face now.

JACK

(shouting) Then don't embarrass me when you're out.

CHRISTINE

(shouting) Nobody is embarrassing you. I was dancing with my cousin, Jack!

JACK pulls his hand back and slaps CHRISTINE in the face. She stumbles back.

JACK

You lying bitch.

CHRISTINE gets up. JACK slaps her again. Grown WILL runs over to JACK and starts hitting him.

WILL   Don't hit my mommy! Don't hit my mommy!

            *JACK leaves the apartment. WILL hugs CHRISTINE. CHRISTINE
            remains calm while WILL cries. MAYA enters.*

MAYA   Mommy, why is Will crying?

CHRISTINE   It's okay, Maya.

            They all embrace. The lights fade out.

            *Lights back on full. We're back in the hospital room with JACK
            and SHELLEY.*

JACK   Will's not coming. Not tomorrow, not ever. He'll never
            come.

            Lights off.

            *Lights back on. We're in WILL and MAYA's apartment. WILL sits
            at his computer typing. There's a knock at the door.*

WILL   Use your key!

            The knock continues.

            For crying out loud, Maya, use your key!

            The knock continues.

            (under his breath) Soldier or not, I'm gonna kick your...

            *WILL opens it. FRANÇOIS, his half-brother, stands in the doorway.
            He's just as tall as WILL, same build mostly, just a lighter com-
            plexion separates the brothers.*

FRANÇOIS   Hey Will.

WILL	Hey.
FRANÇOIS	Can I?
WILL	I'm actually in the middle of a chapter here. It's a bad time.
FRANÇOIS	Please, man, I just need to talk to someone.
WILL	And you came here?
FRANÇOIS	I just need a few minutes please.

WILL lets him in without saying a word. FRANÇOIS enters. This is awkward.

WILL	You want a beer?
FRANÇOIS	Please.

They open up a couple beers. Gentlemanly to each other, but by no means close.

WILL	Sorry to hear about your dad.
FRANÇOIS	No you're not.
WILL	Fair enough, you're right. So, why'd you come here?
FRANÇOIS	He's your dad too.
WILL	Seems to be the line of the week around here. My sister's already given me the run-through. So without being rude, what do you want, François?
FRANÇOIS	I don't know really. My dad's dying and I really don't have anyone going through the same thing besides my sis, but she's halfway across the world. The funny thing is, I know you don't

	care, but you're the only one who can feel what I'm feeling. What it's like to know your father is dying.
WILL	How would I know? I don't have one.
FRANÇOIS	Do you always have to be like that?
WILL	I don't really know how much of a position you're in to tell me what I should be like.
FRANÇOIS	Why? You've had this chip on your shoulder for how long, bro? Don't you think it's time you let it go?
WILL	First of all, you're not my bro. Second, you're treading down some dangerous territory here, kid.
FRANÇOIS	Okay, so yeah, he stayed with my mother. And he raised me and Jessica and he gave us everything we could want and everything we asked for. I'm sorry you didn't get that from him. I am. But he was a good man and he's a better man now and he's sorry for anything he didn't give you. He's dying, man, he's dying and he just wants to have his family around him. Whether you like it or not, you're his son. You are family and you should be there. Okay, he left you and I'm sorry, but bro, deal with it.
WILL	*(irritated)* BECAUSE HE LEFT YOU? You think that's why I hate him? I don't hate him because he left. I hate him because of who he is. What he did to my mother, what he put me and my sister through. No, HE IS NOT MY FATHER! My father died when he abandoned my mother. My father died when I saw how he treated the woman who raised me! To hell with that! To hell with him! Do you know what it's like to see your mom struggle to provide for you and never show how difficult it is for her. I know what it's like to have the lights go off in the apartment and my mom tell us we're just playing a game of hide and seek. To see my mom cooking for us every day, buying us toys and video games on Christmas

when things were hard and she had to worry about rent. Tell me, BRO, what's it like to have your mom push you through the snow when her car broke down and your apartment is still thirty-five minutes away. I know what it's like to sit in a park with my mother and her friends and watch as your beloved Jack, your father, walked by us without acknowledging his own kids. His own kids! And I know what it's like for me, my sister, and my mother to walk into a store and see your saint of a father buying gifts for you and your family like it's nothing, while we're making ends. Making ends... while you guys are living it up! So, don't you dare come in here and try and sell me on who Jack is. I know all I need to know about your father... bro.

FRANÇOIS   Well, I'm sorry he found a family he loved and a woman he loved more than your mother.

        WILL leaps toward FRANÇOIS, knocks over a picture, and in one swift motion grabs FRANÇOIS by his throat.

WILL   My mother or her name will never come out of your mouth again. Do you understand me?

FRANÇOIS   *(muzzled)* Get your hands off me.

WILL   Do you understand me?

FRANÇOIS   I understand you. Now get off me.

WILL   Get the hell out.

        FRANÇOIS walks toward the door.

FRANÇOIS   On second thought, it's better if you don't show up. We don't need your energy around us. Nobody does.

        He leaves. WILL picks up the picture he knocked down. It's a picture of him with Noah and Alison. He stares at it.

WILL	*(to the picture)* Don't look at me like that. What the hell? I'm not like him. I'm not even close to being like him. Dammit, you know that! I won't be.

End of Act II

ACT III

Lights fade on. The EKG beeps. Flashback to a hospital room fifteen years ago. CHRISTINE is in the bed. A teenage MAYA and WILL are in the room. MAYA is standing at the bedside. WILL is seated close by. He barely moves.

MAYA	Mom, please be okay.
CHRISTINE	I will be, honey. It'll all be okay.
MAYA	Promise.
CHRISTINE	I will be okay. Trust me. I know everything.
MAYA	You always say that.
CHRISTINE	It's true. And I know you need to take care of your big brother. He's going to need you.
MAYA	But you're not going anywhere.
CHRISTINE	I know, honey. Just promise me you'll take care of him. He's a bit of a baby, you know.
WILL	Mom, I'm right here. I can hear you.
CHRISTINE	Shhh, I'm talking to your sister.

MAYA smiles.

CHRISTINE   Come here, you big suck.

                   WILL walks over to the bed. A sullen walk.

WILL   Hi Mom.

CHRISTINE   You already said hi to me when you came in.

WILL   I know. I just don't know what to say, Mom.

CHRISTINE   You just continue to do what you've always done. Be a great
                   son who's always made me proud. I want you to look after
                   your younger sister. Listen to Grandma and Grandpa. They're
                   your parents now and they'll be good to you like always. And
                   you just make us all proud like you have. Never give up, pro-
                   tect and love your family, and pray every day, Will. Every day
                   and always give thanks. God has big plans for you, son.

WILL   How do you know?

CHRISTINE   You don't know yet? I just told your sister, I know everything.

                   WILL smiles.

WILL   I know, Mom.

CHRISTINE   Good.

WILL   I'm sad, Mom.

CHRISTINE   Well, you promise me you'll do everything I told you and
                   you'll make me very happy. I promise I'll never be sad again if
                   you do that.

WILL   Okay, I promise.

CHRISTINE   Good. Now promise me you'll forgive.

WILL	Forgive who?

CHRISTINE	Forgive anyone who hurts you. I don't want you to ever have hate in your heart. You understand?

WILL	But...

CHRISTINE	No but. Nobody. I want you to love and forgive... always, son.

WILL	Why?

CHRISTINE	Because I said so.

WILL looks down. The EKG continues to beep.

And because when you go on with hate in your heart, all you carry is a burden. A burden and a weight that stays with you and grows with you. I used to have that. I let it go. I let it go because that person you're hating is living his or her life and you're stuck with the burden, and it can bring you down, Will. Okay. So promise. For me.

WILL	Okay. I promise, Mom.

CHRISTINE	Good. Now wipe the snot out of your nose. It looks nasty!

Laughs from all.

I love you two.

MAYA	I love you too.

WILL	We love you too, Mom.

Lights fade out.

Lights back on. We're in the hospital. The EKG beeps. JACK is in bed, SHELLEY is seated. MAYA is in the room sipping a cup of tea.

SHELLEY   It was good to see Samantha and her husband.

JACK   You always call him "her husband." Why don't you say his name? Is that how you refer to me? "My husband," like I'm some nameless chap?

SHELLEY   *(laughs)* Don't be ridiculous. I call you, "my big boo boo" and François is "little boo boo."

JACK   You're a moron.

SHELLEY   But you love it.

JACK   I love you.

SHELLEY   I love you too.

They kiss. Short.

MAYA   Couldn't you have germs that could make him even more sick? I mean we should be taking every precaution, right?

JACK looks at MAYA suspiciously.

It's true though.

JACK   I'll take a germ from her any day.

Another kiss.

WILL enters.

WILL   So you are capable of emotion?

	MAYA stands up. She's shocked, almost as much as SHELLEY. JACK looks over.
MAYA	Will, I knew you'd come.
WILL	What's with the champagne?
SHELLEY	It's your father's birthday, Will. It's so good of you to make it.
	Silence. Both JACK and WILL just look at each other. Motionless.
SHELLEY	Maya, maybe we should give these two some time?
MAYA	Shelley, maybe YOU should give US some time?
	Awkward. SHELLEY kisses JACK.
SHELLEY	I'll be outside, honey.
MAYA	Will, I'll give you guys time.
WILL	Don't leave me.
MAYA	I won't. I'll be right outside the door.
	MAYA hugs WILL.
	I'm glad you came.
	She exits.
JACK	Hi Will.
	Lights fade. A spotlight falls on WILL, all else is dark. WILL stands for a moment. He exhales.
WILL	Gone, The word we use to describe

Those who have left us,
Left us alone,
Left us scarred,
Or simply just left,
And all we have is a vision
Of what could have been,
Marred by the decision
To leave the responsibility
That should have been,
See, we often show our love for those close to us
When it is far too late,
I cannot begin to comprehend the passing of a father,
But I refuse to commemorate the memory
Of one who left,
You see,
I have a heart that bleeds for those I love,
But for you, my dead father,
My heart is of stone
Stronger than the will of a king or a slave's backbone,
Overstand, that I shed tears for those who sacrificed for me,
Not the one who picked up and left
My sister and me,
With a beautiful mother who suffered silently,
Putting her dreams on hold,
To raise a young girl into a lady,
And a young boy
To set an example for all men
All because you decided
To walk away from the test,
After all the ink had left your pen,
You see,
Unlike you,
I could never sit still
And listen to the tears of a woman
Asking me how she's going to pay all these bills,
And yes,
I've made mistakes in my space,
But to a woman,

I would never let my hand meet her face,
Far from perfect I am,
But I am striving to be,
Better than the outcome of my possible destiny,
I am blessed with a grandfather
Who schooled me,
Educated me,
On the importance of family,
He is my real father
And my grandma
My second mother to me,
So, for me, nothing comes before blood
And the strength of unity,
I look into the eyes of my son
And I know for him I will die,
His smile is enough to make
My stone heart cry,
But for you, my dead father
Gone, but not forgotten,
Your legacy will die with me,
I am what you could never be,
A man,
A son,
A father,
And I will raise up my seed to be better than me,
Or at least,
Pretty close,
I'm guilty in my own way,
I've ignored the mother of my son,
And that mistake I'm changing now,
This is the dawning of a new day,
Becoming like the man who left me,
To that, you will never see that day,
My son,
I say, "no way,"
Will I let you know pain from my words and actions,
And if I have
I apologize in the most profound way,

So I stand here,
In the memory of my mother who raised me,
Put the work in
To mould me
With love and spirituality,
I am eternally grateful,
So, I lift my hand and toast
Not to my dead father,
I've let go of that ghost,
This drink I hold now
Is for the woman I love most,
And that is
My living mother.

Lights fade off.

End of Act III.

End of play.

Behind the Scenes
With Laurence Anthony

Laurence Anthony's resume as an actor is filled with such national TV hits as *The Border* and *Degrassi: The Next Generation*. He's been writing short stories, plays, and comic books since he was eight years old. His short story "The Lido Deck" was included in the best-selling book LAID: *Young People's Experiences with Sex in an Easy Access Culture*.

He has enjoyed being the creator and host of *One Night Only*, a showcase featuring singers, musicians, and poets in Toronto, and he loves his venture into writing the very contemporary play *Toast*.

A general audition for actors brought Anthony to the Obsidian Theatre Company's attention. He recited some of his own work for Philip Akin. This is often discouraged by theatres; they don't want to know if you can write, but if you can act. For Obsidian both skills are an asset and both were welcomed in Laurence Anthony. He was asked to be in the Playwrights Unit and was given the opportunity to grow from writing for his solo voice to creating a work in which several actors could play great roles.

The best thing about writing plays for Laurence is the sense of the endless possibilities it affords. He revels in "the exploration of new characters, creating an entirely new world, and playing with the possibilities that exist." He continues, "when writing a play, you take on the role of a creator, of a god, and these characters can do whatever you choose. It's also a great way to explore the emotions and feelings you, as a playwright, have inside."

The least appealing aspect of being a playwright for Anthony is perfectionism, he always wants the scripts to be better. "You can never step in the same river twice and it's always changing. Deadlines are also horrible, because they're necessary, but add a tremendous amount of pressure."

In the future Anthony would like to take on some more of those endless possibilities. He would like to expand *Toast*, begin work on some children's stories, and start work on a novel.

For Anthony, Obsidian is a constant source of useful information and connections that contribute to his growth as an artist and as a person. Connections he regards as a life raft in an isolated craft.

RELATIONSHIPS
IN THEIR UPS AND DOWNS

LATE
By Marcia Johnson

voice give just granite company black theatre
OBSIDIAN ENCOURAGEMENT GLASS STRONG JET
SPACE voice give just GRANITE COMPANY BLACK
THEATRE OBSIDIAN ENCOURAGEMENT GLASS
HARD STRONG SPACE JET voice give JUST
GRANITE COMPANY BLACK THEATRE
OBSIDIAN ENCOURAGEMENT GLASS SPAC

CHARACTERS

Donna

Carol

For Philip Akin, Artistic Director of Obsidian Theatre Company

DONNA is setting a table for two in a breakfast nook. Coffee is brewing and there is a teapot from which she pours tea into her own cup. It's an unhurried, easygoing atmosphere.

DONNA   Cam, we're out of honey. Is brown sugar okay?

There's no response.

(mockingly) Not at all, Donna. Brown sugar's fine.

She puts a teaspoon of sugar into Cam's cup.

(back to normal way of speaking) I'll get some later today. Is there anything else we need?

DONNA goes to the cupboards, opening two doors so she can get a good view.

Rice, pasta, tuna…

She closes the cupboard doors and opens the fridge.

Butter, eggs, milk, lettuce, fruit… meat— Everything. Okay, I'll go later.

DONNA sits down to a bowl of cereal and her cup of tea. She smiles to herself.

Mmmm. It was great this morning. Blame me if you're late. Tell Doug you had to kill a spider for me. No. A mouse. They're harder to catch. Touch wood.

> *She knocks on the table. There is another knock at the door. DONNA's not quite sure if she's hearing things. Another knock. This sets her into action.*

Coming!

> *She clears Cam's bowl, coffee cup, and flatware and deposits them into the sink. She checks the table, goes to the door, and opens it. A woman (CAROL) is standing on the stoop holding a beautiful moth orchid.*

CAROL   Oh hello. Donna?

DONNA   Yes.

CAROL   I'm from downstairs.

DONNA   What happened to Stu?

CAROL   I've been subletting from him for the past month.

DONNA   Oh, I'd heard something about that. Is anything wrong?

CAROL   No. No. I brought this for you.

DONNA   Thank you. It's beautiful.

CAROL   I've been meaning to come by.

DONNA   It's very nice of you.

CAROL   Well. I just wanted to pay my… to express my… Oh I never know what to say in these… I'll just go.

DONNA   No. It's fine. Please, come in.

CAROL   I didn't want to intrude.

DONNA   You're not.

CAROL   Are you sure? I thought I heard you talking to someone.

DONNA   No. It's just me. Please, come in.

CAROL   All right then.

>   *CAROL enters.*

DONNA   I'll just put it in the window.

>   *She does.*

CAROL   You're lucky you get so much sun.

DONNA   Yes. Would you like a cup of tea?

CAROL   I thought I smelled coffee.

DONNA   Right. There's coffee too. But I'm out of milk.

CAROL   Oh, I take it black.

DONNA   That's lucky. Please make yourself at home.

>   *DONNA takes a cup from the cupboard and pours coffee. CAROL
>   sits at the table.*

CAROL   I was interrupting your breakfast.

DONNA   No, I'm done.

>   *DONNA puts her bowl in the sink.*

CAROL	There's still cereal in the bowl.
DONNA	Couldn't finish.
CAROL	It's important to keep your strength up.
DONNA	I know.

Both women sip from their cups. There's an awkwardness.

CAROL	I've actually had that orchid for a week waiting for the right moment to give it to you. You had so many visitors.
DONNA	It felt like hundreds.
CAROL	Yes, well… I noticed one of the blossoms looking a bit droopy this morning so I thought: "This must be the day." It wouldn't have lasted much longer in the basement. I don't know how Stuart stands it being so dark down there.
DONNA	He travels a lot.
CAROL	That probably helps.
DONNA	You had the right idea. Everyone else gave me cut flowers that just died on me. Ironic.
CAROL	They meant well.
DONNA	I know.
CAROL	How long has it been?
DONNA	Three weeks.
CAROL	How old was he?
DONNA	Twenty-six.

CAROL	Good lord.
DONNA	I know.
CAROL	I'm so sorry.
DONNA	Thank you. How much longer are you staying downstairs?
CAROL	I leave tonight.
DONNA	Oh.
CAROL	I've been here all this time and this is the first time we've met. I'm sorry.
DONNA	I'm touched that you wanted to meet me at all.
CAROL	I know I would have regretted it if I hadn't at least said "I'm sorry for your loss," and I am. I really am.

CAROL begins to cry.

DONNA	Oh. Don't...
CAROL	I'm so sorry.
DONNA	It's all right. It's all right... uh...
CAROL	Carol.
DONNA	Carol.
CAROL	You're keeping it together so well.

DONNA puts a box of tissues on the table and CAROL helps herself to a few. It's very messy crying.

DONNA	You think so?

CAROL   You're not in your pyjamas. This place is spotless. I've been
             downstairs sitting in clutter all month crying every day.

DONNA   Not because of me.

CAROL   No. My boyfriend and I split up. I needed somewhere to stay.

DONNA   I'm sorry.

CAROL   Don't feel sorry for me. You of all people. My ex is a jerk. He
             isn't dead.

DONNA   You've found an apartment?

CAROL   Yeah. In Calgary. I'm running away. How pathetic is that?

DONNA   It's not. You're making a fresh start.

CAROL   How can you be so nice to me? *(doesn't give her time to answer)*
             This wasn't how I expected this to go.

DONNA   It's going just fine.

CAROL   You're so strong.

DONNA   I don't have much choice.

CAROL   That's a healthy way of looking at it.

DONNA   It's the only way.

CAROL   Are you going to move?

DONNA   No. I love this place. It reminds me so much of him.

CAROL   Doesn't that make it worse?

DONNA   I don't want to forget him.

CAROL	That wouldn't happen.
DONNA	I feel like I'm already forgetting some things.
CAROL	You are?
DONNA	The way he touched me…

DONNA appears to drift off.

CAROL	I shouldn't be making you talk about this.
DONNA	Does it make you uncomfortable?
CAROL	Well, no—
DONNA	It's been interesting seeing how different people deal with death. Some of them are just terrified. They drop off a card and their dying flowers and run away like they're afraid it'll catch. Like they're waiting until I get out of quarantine.
CAROL	Maybe they want to give you your space.
DONNA	Maybe. There have been a few people who act as though I should be over it already. They'll talk about the weather, the Oscars, anything but the dead elephant in the room.
CAROL	How sad.
DONNA	They're better than the grief junkies. I hate the way they cry and cry. They want me to cry with them. If I don't shed enough tears, they just keep on picking until they get me going.
CAROL	Is that what I'm doing?
DONNA	No. You're being very respectful.
CAROL	I'm not sure what to say now.

DONNA	Whatever you want.
CAROL	What do they say? The grief junkies, when they "pick."
DONNA	Oh, they remind me that I'll never have children with him.
CAROL	That's terrible.
DONNA	They like telling me that I'm a widow at twenty-eight. Things that I already know.
CAROL	Why would they do that?
DONNA	I don't know, but it just flows out of them. They can't stop. See, you're not so bad.
CAROL	I guess not.
DONNA	Feel better?
CAROL	Yes.
DONNA	Good.
CAROL	Is this what you've been doing?
DONNA	What?
CAROL	Making everyone feel better?
DONNA	It makes it easier for them to leave me alone.
CAROL	But it's not about them.
DONNA	It is a little. I'm not the only one who lost Cam.

> *This was a difficult thing for* DONNA *to say. She stands and becomes very focused on keeping busy.*

Let me get some more coffee for you. Would you like some toast?

CAROL Donna.

CAROL stands and opens her arms to her.

DONNA What are you doing?

CAROL Let me hold you.

DONNA Why?

CAROL Because you don't have anyone to lean on.

DONNA That's sweet but I'm all—

CAROL Sometimes it's easier with a stranger than with the people closest to you.

CAROL moves in closer with her arms open.

DONNA You don't have to do this.

CAROL I know.

CAROL envelops DONNA in her arms. DONNA is rigid in her embrace.

DONNA Okay. Thanks.

DONNA tries to extricate herself. CAROL won't let her go.

CAROL Donna, let me help. Let go. Let go.

DONNA I am.

CAROL No, you're not.

DONNA	I can't.
CAROL	Yes, you can.
DONNA	What makes you think you can handle it?

> *DONNA pulls herself away and puts distance between her and CAROL.*

CAROL	Let's ease into it.
DONNA	How?
CAROL	Well, start with something a little removed and work our way to the real thing.
DONNA	Something removed from my husband's death?
CAROL	Something connected to it. Like the flowers.
DONNA	I don't know.
CAROL	Sit down with me. Please.

> *CAROL sits. DONNA reluctantly joins her.*

	Did you know that there are over nine hundred species of orchids?
DONNA	No.
CAROL	What do you think about that?
DONNA	It's… pretty amazing. I'm sorry. I don't know how—
CAROL	And those species tend to have their own varieties.
DONNA	Wow?

CAROL   Come on, Donna. You can do this.

DONNA   Why do you want to?

CAROL   Please, I've been wasting my energy for a month. Let me be useful.

DONNA   But I don't know anything about orchids.

CAROL   You must know something.

DONNA   Do they grow in the rainforest?

CAROL   Let's say yes.

DONNA   But, that doesn't make sense. Don't they need a lot of light? How can the sun reach them on the forest floor?

CAROL   Don't they grow on tree trunks?

DONNA   Yes! I saw an IMAX film about the rainforest. They were growing sideways out of these huge trees. Hey, I'm doing it!

CAROL   Good. What else?

DONNA   Well, there was this praying mantis, I think, that evolved to look just like one of the varieties to protect itself from predators.

CAROL   Like camouflage?

DONNA   Right.

CAROL   Good. Keep going.

DONNA   Oh, and I think that they feed off the nutrients from the trees that they grow on. The trees are actually...

CAROL   Don't stop there, Donna. The trees are actually...

DONNA	The trees are actually dying. The orchids thrive on decay.
CAROL	Oh.
DONNA	Everything leads back to death.
CAROL	Oh God.
DONNA	Nice try.
CAROL	Do you want me to go?
DONNA	You must have a lot of packing to do.
CAROL	I'm shipping a lot of it. Jim's agreed to pay for it.
DONNA	That's nice of him.
CAROL	I don't even want it. Who wants memories from a failed relationship? Sorry.
DONNA	My relationship didn't fail.
CAROL	You're right. God.
DONNA	Things will be better in Calgary.
CAROL	I hope so. I think meeting you has helped me.
DONNA	How?
CAROL	Whenever I feel tempted to feel sorry for myself, I'll think of how well you're coping.
DONNA	I really don't deserve your admiration.
CAROL	Yes, you do.

DONNA   No, I don't.

CAROL   You shouldn't feel guilty about moving on.

DONNA   I don't see that happening for some time.

CAROL   It's all right, Donna. You don't have to pretend.

DONNA   You're not making any sense.

CAROL   If you don't want to talk about him, that's your business, but I just hope he isn't taking advantage of you.

DONNA   Who?

CAROL   Your new boyfriend. I hear you talking to him all the time.

DONNA   You're mistaken.

CAROL   Don't you ever hear me crying sometimes?

DONNA   Yeah. So?

CAROL   I can hear you too.

        DONNA freezes.

DONNA   What have you heard?

CAROL   He doesn't have to hide on my account.

DONNA   There's no one else here. I could never bring anyone else into that bed.

CAROL   But I hear you in the mornings.

DONNA   Oh my God.

CAROL	And why would you make coffee when you're drinking tea?
DONNA	For the smell. Cam loved his coffee. It makes me feel like he's going to walk out of the bedroom any minute.
CAROL	Really? There's no one in there?
DONNA	Most mornings, he would wake up ahead of the alarm. Then he'd wake me up. It was so perfect. Waking up to him caressing me, loving me. After three years, we were still on our honeymoon. Our bodies seemed to be made for each other. We'd hold each other so tight that I felt like I could burrow into him. It's where I wanted to live.
CAROL	This is really personal.
DONNA	This is what you wanted!
CAROL	All right. Take it easy.
DONNA	Do you want to hear the rest or not?
CAROL	Yes, Donna.
DONNA	Okay. He'd take a shower. I'd fall asleep again and wake up with the alarm. I'd put the coffee on and he'd take his first sip while he was still in his towel. I lived for those moments every morning. Now, I wake up before the alarm and lie perfectly still, hoping that his hands will start touching me. If I don't roll over, I won't see that he's not there. Every morning, I lie in bed waiting for his touch. Like it's all been a bad dream. How's that for strong?
CAROL	You poor thing.
DONNA	That's more like it.
	Anything's better than your stupid admiration.

CAROL	I was only trying to be nice.
DONNA	I don't need anyone to be nice.
CAROL	I'll go.

CAROL opens the door.

DONNA	Just like everybody else.
CAROL	At least now you know that the sound works both ways.
DONNA	Carol, wait… I'm sorry.
CAROL	It's all right.
DONNA	No. It isn't.
CAROL	You were due for a good rant.
DONNA	It's no excuse.
CAROL	Have you thought of getting help?
DONNA	You're not the first person to suggest it.
CAROL	There are people who specialize in dealing with loss.
DONNA	Do you think I could learn how not to snap when well-meaning people try to give me some comfort?
CAROL	Oh, that's normal. It's… the other thing—
DONNA	The pretending to have sex with my dead husband thing?
CAROL	Will you think about it?
DONNA	Why couldn't you just let it go?

CAROL   I don't know.

DONNA   I don't want to lose him.

CAROL   You won't.

DONNA   Are you sure?

CAROL   How could you?

> CAROL *takes a business card out of her pocket.*

I've been hanging on to this for a while.

DONNA   *(taking the card)* Grief counsellor.

CAROL   I hear she's really good.

DONNA   Thank you for talking to me. I mean for really talking to me.

> CAROL *moves in to hug her again.*

(softly) No.

CAROL   I'm just going to the store. Do you need anything?

DONNA   No.

CAROL   No?

DONNA   Thanks anyway.

CAROL   Okay then. Bye Donna.

DONNA   Bye Carol. I'll take really good care of the orchid.

> CAROL *exits.* DONNA *closes the door after her.* DONNA *picks up the orchid and looks at it admiringly.*

That can't be right about them living off decay. I think it's called a moth. Such a plain name for such a beautiful flower.

After a moment she speaks louder, as though to someone in the next room.

I said the name doesn't suit it. I will not kill it. You're the one who overwatered the philodendron. Do you know how hard it is to kill one of those? I'll water it once a week and mist it every day. Aren't you going to be late for work? Cam? Cam?

DONNA *exits to the bedroom. She squeals in delight as though being grabbed playfully.*

(from off) You're so going to be late. *(as though kissing)* Mmmm.

The end.

BEHIND THE SCENES
WITH MARCIA JOHNSON

Marcia Johnson has participated in playwrights' groups at the Obsidian Theatre Company, Theatre Passe Muraille, the Siminovitch Prize Playwriting Master Class with Carole Fréchette, a musical theatre master class with William Finn at the Canadian Stage Company, Canadian Stage's BASH residency, Tapestry New Opera's Composer-Librettist Laboratory (Lib Lab), and the Ontario Arts Council Playwright Residencies at Blyth Festival and Roseneath Theatre.

Marcia teaches an introduction to playwriting class at Sheridan Technical Institute in Oakville, is on the board of Theatre Ontario, is a member of Playwrights' Workshop Montréal, and is Chair of the Women's Caucus of the Playwrights Guild of Canada. She has also been a professional actor in Toronto since 1983. Most recently, she originated roles in *The Real McCoy* by Andrew Moodie and *I Grow Old* (part of *The Gladstone Variations*) by Julie Tepperman.

Her most cherished acting assignment was playing Mary Eleanora Delaney in *The Real McCoy*. She also enjoyed writing the libretto for the suspenseful short opera *My Mother's Ring*. Finally, reaching back in time, Marcia fondly remembers playing the Fairy God-robot in her grade four production of *Space Cinderella*.

Late, as several of the other plays in this anthology, was inspired by visual arts. Johnson's inspiration was a painting by Lisa Herrera. It is of a sleeping nude woman. "What caught my eye was the smile on her face. I wondered if she was dreaming or was waiting for her lover. Then I imagined that her lover was not returning and that, in her waking moments, she'd forgotten that fact."

Marcia cites her fondness for total control as the best thing about writing plays. "I actually have control over what is being said and done. I can write, rewrite, and get insight from other people. Then I can hear it spoken by talented actors. Playwriting is a kind of redress for the awful social blunders I have caused. It is also an artistic vengeance where I get to (through my characters) say the absolutely right thing. Even if it's the wrong thing, it's by design and absolutely necessary for the plot."

The worst thing about writing plays, says Johnson, is second-guessing herself after the "final" draft.

Johnson believes the contributions Obsidian Theatre Company has made to the Canadian theatre scene to be considerable: "Obsidian is opening the eyes of audiences to the notion that Black writers are as diverse, talented, and unique as any other writers. Philip Akin, in particular, encourages writers to stretch the boundaries, to not only write what may be expected of a Black writer. He is drawing from and helping to create a pool of excellent Canadian playwrights."

Marcia Johnson concludes that she loves writing but is an actor first. "I would never have written my first play if it hadn't been to create a leading role for myself."

Bus Stop
By Dian Marie Bridge

voice give just granite company black theatre
OBSIDIAN ENCOURAGEMENT GLASS STRONG JET
SPACE VOICE GIVE JUST GRANITE COMPANY BLACK
THEATRE OBSIDIAN ENCOURAGEMENT GLASS
HARD STRONG SPACE JET VOICE GIVE JUST
GRANITE COMPANY BLACK THEATRE
OBSIDIAN ENCOURAGEMENT GLASS SPAC

CHARACTERS

Francie: twenty-four-year-old woman, dressed in a young/fashionable outfit. She is slightly awkward in her clothes.

Tom: twenty-six-year-old man, wearing loose jeans, a buttoned-down white shirt, and high-top runners.

A bus-stop shelter on the corner of a busy urban side street. The street is lined with cafés and boutiques. FRANCIE is waiting inside the bus shelter, sitting on the bench. It is a late spring evening.

FRANCIE   *(tilting her head to one side)* Hello? *(pause, a bit annoyed)* Hi. *(pause)* Okaaay. Hi, I'm Francie. *(tilts her head in the other direction)* You don't know what you are talking about! *(laughs out loud)* Francine? Francine is the name of an '80s disco dancer... Oh yes I do have moves!

TOM enters the shelter, running in from across the street.

Oh, you name it, electric slide, hustle, shuffle. *(laughs again)* Yeah board!

FRANCIE takes notice of TOM, looks at him, and then decides that he is not the man she is waiting for. TOM takes a step away from her and sits on the other end of the bench.

Yeah, well I am answering my phone, so what does that tell you? No, no, no plan B necessary. No. I said no. I swear if you ever try to talk me into this again... *(pause)* No, I'm still here. *(pause)* Yes. Girl, I don't know. *(pause)* I know! It's totally weird. Not a coffee shop or a mall, but public transit, and I don't even know what he looks like. I feel like I have been in a fish bowl for an hour. Something like ten buses have passed. *(pause)* I'll give him fifteen more minutes.

TOM laughs.

I kinda have an audience, so I will check you later, okay? Bye.

FRANCIE moves closer to TOM.

TOM   Sorry, I didn't mean to be cause for you to cut your conversation short.

FRANCIE   Life is readily on display these days anyway. I was finished anyways.

TOM   That's what you get with living in the city, hey? Heck, living in our time. You know, I updated my status and cleaned up my profile and then for the next two days I got messages from people telling me how sorry they were that I got dumped, and what a great guy I was. I mean am. What a great guy I am.

FRANCIE   I am sure you are just fine. At least you are here and talking to me, unlike some others.

TOM   Talking is not a strong suit for most.

FRANCIE   I'm sorry, but I think that that is garbage.

TOM   No, it's totally true. We are very visual creatures.

FRANCIE   Yeah, I have heard that, but I don't know if I buy it.

TOM   Well, take you for instance. You look nice. *(He looks over her hair and clothes.)*

FRANCIE   Thanks. And?

TOM   It's amazing how small those things are.

FRANCIE   What things? What are you talking about? Are you a pervert? My breasts, are you talking about my breasts?

TOM	I'm sorry. I thought that you were on the phone when I came in here. You were talking to someone on the phone, were you not?
FRANCIE	Were you listening to my conversation?
TOM	No, I just thought that you were—well, I mean at first, I thought that you were just talking to yourself, and then I realized that you were talking to someone. Your Bluetooth. They make them really small now.
FRANCIE	Yes they do. Well, aren't you a brave one for taking a seat next to a "crazy" woman talking to herself in a shelter.
TOM	They make those things really small now. When I was crossing the street you looked kinda crazy. I mean you are very expressive with your hands. Kinda doesn't match your voice.
FRANCIE	Oh, wow.
TOM	We are all a bit crazy though.
FRANCIE	Not all of us.
TOM	Well, to some degree, sure we are. Functioning doesn't mean that you got all your shit sorted. I mean, who knows why people do the things that they do or say the things that they say half the time. I mean really, we are all living in total opposition to the natural order of the world and getting away with it. Don't you think that that makes mankind kinda nuts?
FRANCIE	Are you okay?
TOM	I'm sorry, you are a pretty lady; I get nervous.
FRANCIE	(getting up from the bench and pretending to look for a bus) Um, thanks. It doesn't look like my bus is coming, so I'm just going to leave you know.

TOM   Oh shit, I'm sorry. Did that totally weird you out? That did! Sorry sorry. But I think it's true. I will shut up now. Want a cookie? *(He pulls a giant chocolate-chip cookie from his bag.)*

FRANCIE   No thank you.

TOM   I got it from Café Sylvia across the street. I work there. You look really nice. Are you waiting for someone?

FRANCIE   Café Sylvia? Across the street. I bet it's nice and cozy in there.

TOM   I work there, so I kinda think of it as a dark hole. You have been here for a while.

FRANCIE   Yeah, I think my bus got cancelled or something.

TOM   I think you might be waiting for someone.

FRANCIE   That obvious? I am so never doing this again.

TOM   He's late?

FRANCIE   Just a bit, yeah.

TOM   How late?

FRANCIE   What? Why do you want to know that?

TOM   I think women and men have a different perception of time is all.

FRANCIE   Um, three is three. Not three thirty, and definitely not three forty-five.

TOM   It's three thirty now. Were you supposed to meet at three?

FRANCIE   Yes. *(pause)* And he is a half-hour late… and I think I don't want to have this conversation anymore.

TOM	Sorry, *(pause)* it's just that when you were talking to your friend a minute ago, you said you had been waiting for an hour.
FRANCIE	What are you, like a reporter or writer… or what? *(pause)* Yes, I have been here for an hour.
TOM	Why did you come so early? If your date was at three…
FRANCIE	Yes, my date was at three. I came early because I don't know the area very well and this particular man asked me to meet him here. At this bus stop. I was being respectful of his time and planned to be a few minutes early, and turns out that here was much closer than I thought.
TOM	And now you're pissed?
FRANCIE	I am pissed because I am here in a bus stop with a barista who is badgering me when all I am really trying is to keep some degree of pride about me. Now, thank you for your interest in this particular humiliation, but I will be taking my leave of you now. Excuse me.
TOM	Francie. *(pause)* I'm sorry I was late.
FRANCIE	Wow. Are you for real? Are you freaking kidding me with this? What, do you have cameras hidden on the street somewhere? You know what? You have a fantastic rest of your day now. I am going home.
TOM	I'm sorry, I'm sorry. I work across the street there and my shift went over. I saw when you first got here, but you were so early that I didn't think it was you. And then it just looked like you were talking to yourself the whole time.
FRANCIE	I was on the phone.
TOM	Yeah, I know that now. I just had to find out. I mean at first it was like, "This chick is totally wacked," but then I got interested.

FRANCIE	Well, it's me. Ta da. You had a look and now I am going home.
TOM	No, no, come on. I planned a really fun afternoon.
FRANCIE	I really don't care what you planned. You just told me that you have been watching me for the past hour and I don't know what that sounds like in Tom world, but to me it's pretty fucked up. I mean, I knew that I would meet some weird guys in my time, but seriously? You watched me for an hour.
TOM	I know it sounds fucked up, but it's just that you were so interesting to watch. I mean, you were all light and nervous at first. Just primping, you fixed your hair something like four times. You look great by the way. Then you got kind of annoyed. You started to stare at people and shut them down. You started to look panicked.
	I don't know why I picked a bus stop. Transitory, transitions, moving or something. I was going to take you to the ROM. I know. It's 'cause it was right across the street and in case you didn't show I would not be humiliated in front of my co-workers. Okay. That good enough for you?
FRANCIE	You know you can get help for that. Seriously.
TOM	Oh yeah. Okay. But you are the one who was willing to wait for a phantom. You should take your own advice.
FRANCIE	Do you have any idea what it is like for a single woman to be waiting at a bus stop for a man who she has no idea what he looks like? You know how many people have stared at me while the 52 bus passed me six times? Would it ever occur to you that a woman sitting by herself in a bus shelter would look out of place? I have been propositioned twice while waiting for you. I have been asked by a very sweet old lady if I was lost, and all to meet a stalker.
TOM	You sound whiny. You hungry? I have that cookie.

FRANCIE	Are you for real?
TOM	I'll let you leave if you tell me why you waited.
FRANCIE	You'll let me leave?
TOM	Okay, so obviously we both are feeling humiliated right about now. I think you should get your blood sugar up. I was going to take you to this really great noodle house, but for some reason, I don't think that you want to go with me anymore. So all I can do is offer you this cookie.
FRANCIE	I do not need your permission to go anywhere.
TOM	Yeah I know, but here you are waiting for it.

> *FRANCIE stares at him. She is furious.*

So why did you really wait?

> *TOM sits on the bench. After a while, FRANCIE sits beside him, staring straight out to the street. After a long while she turns to him and gives him a kiss on the cheek. She is crying.*

You are gonna be okay. We are all going to be okay. Cookie?

> *FRANCIE breaks a big piece of the cookie off and begins to eat. She exits.*

Behind the Scenes
With Dian Marie Bridge

Dian Marie Bridge is a theatre artist living and working in Toronto. She is a participant in the Stratford Shakespeare Festival's Michael Langham Workshops for Classical Direction, was the Intern Artistic Director at Obsidian Theatre Company in 2009, and was the editor of CanPlay Magazine from 2007 to 2009. She is also a founding member of Toronto's Cric Crac Collective and Vancouver's 4large Heads Collective. She has worked as a director, playwright, and producer throughout Canada and in the US.

Dian Marie's three favourite credits all involve directing. She is most proud of her time as an Intern Director at Obsidian. Another highlight was serving as Assistant Director for *Jacques Brel Is Alive and Well and Living In Paris* at the Stratford Shakespeare Festival. She also values her gig as assistant director on *'da Kink in my hair* for Mirvish Productions.

One of the tasks given to Obsidian Playwrights Unit members was writing a play based on an incident in the news. This was the trigger for Bridge's *Bus Stop*. Her imagination was sparked by a clipping about whales being separated during migration.

When asked what the best thing about writing plays is, Dian Marie responds: "Efficiency in language and clarity of story is most beautiful when it allows performers to imbue a space with life that is as vivid as the imagination. I will be working towards that my entire life."

Not surprisingly, she believes the worst thing about writing plays is the opposite: "When you know that you are forcing a plot/line/character to go somewhere that it wouldn't go naturally, ultimately you know that yours is the losing side of that struggle, because it will ring false."

Looking towards future accomplishments, Dian Marie will be directing a short workshop presentation of *Julius Caesar* as part of the Michael Langham Workshop at the Stratford Festival, which she sees as a pivotal experience.

With regards to the contribution Obsidian Theatre has made, both for her personal development and to Canadian theatre as a whole, Bridge observes: "Obsidian has been instrumental in my development as a theatre artist and for many emerging Black artists. From being the first director to go through their Mentor Apprentice Training Program, one of the participants in the inaugural Playwrights Units, and finally as Intern Artistic Director, Obsidian and Philip have been a constant support and a place full of mentors and inspiration. "

GROUP
BY AISHA SASHA JOHN

voice give just granite company black theatre

OBSIDIAN ENCOURAGEMENT GLASS STRONG JET

SPACE VOICE GIVE JUST GRANITE COMPANY BLACK

THEATRE OBSIDIAN ENCOURAGEMENT GLASS

HARD STRONG SPACE JET VOICE GIVE JUST

GRANITE COMPANY BLACK THEATRE

OBSIDIAN ENCOURAGEMENT GLASS SPAC

Characters

Cassidy/Sunrise: A short-story writer.

Mila/Rosa: Cassidy's best friend and roommate.

Cameron/Blue Boy: Mutual friend of Cassidy and Mila.

Dr. Sheila: Played alternately by Mila and Blue Boy

Setting

The living room of an apartment Cassidy and Mila share. Set is minimal: two chairs, a table with random junk, and a couch.

CASSIDY   Guys, thanks so much for agreeing to do this. I need it. I need your help. My imagination has its limits. Mila, I'm going to get you to wear this sundress. Cameron, can you put on these tights?

CAMERON   We have to wear costumes. Is that necessary?

CASSIDY   Yes. It will help you get into character.

MILA   Where's the script?

CASSIDY   There is no script. If I had a script I wouldn't need you. Duh. I'll give you guys the premise. And then we'll all improvise and hopefully it will be good and I can just steal it and have an end for my short story. Ta-dahh!

CAMERON   We better be getting credit.

CASSIDY   Don't be silly.

MILA   Improvise? Improvising is so boring.

CASSIDY   Complaining is boring, Mila. Improvising is huge fun.

MILA   As long as I get to the laundromat before it closes.

CASSIDY   Yeah. So what we're improvising is a group therapy session: Dr. Sheila's Tuesday Night Group Therapy. One of us will be the therapist, Dr. Sheila, and the other two will play the patients.

CAMERON	Let me guess. You're playing Dr. Sheila.
CASSIDY	Actually, we all will. We'll rotate. Smartass.
CAMERON	Group therapy, huh? Then why do I have to wear these tights?
CASSIDY	Because your character wears tights. Duh.
CAMERON	Why does my character wear tights?
CASSIDY	Because that's how I wrote him. He's a cyclist, actually. A courier. But I don't have any bike shorts.
CAMERON	Hey! I ride a bike!
CASSIDY	Yeah, and so does half of Toronto. He's not based on you, relax.
CAMERON	But I would never wear bike shorts.
CASSIDY	And your name isn't Blue Boy, either.
CAMERON	This guy's name is Blue Boy?
CASSIDY	Yes. Deal.
MILA	Fuck, is this going to be weird? What's my character's name?
CASSIDY	Rosa.
MILA	Sweet!
CAMERON	And yours?
CASSIDY	Sunrise.
CAMERON	Oh God.

CASSIDY	I'm working with primary colours, okay. Assface.
MILA	Can we start?
CASSIDY	Yes. "Dr. Sheila's Tuesday Night Group Therapy" take one. Mila, why don't you start? You be Dr. Sheila first.
CAMERON	How come she gets a normal name? And where's your costume, Cass?
MILA	Shush! So, I'm Dr. Sheila? I have no idea what I'm doing here.
CASSIDY	I'm wearing it, dumbass. Do whatever you want, Mila. Honestly. I don't care. Feel free to just completely make it up. But maybe it would be nice if you could include some hypnosis. You know, hypnotherapy. Or not. Whatever. It's up to you. Really, feel free to do "therapist" in whatever way naturally comes to you. I don't want to give you too much guidance. Any guidance, really. Part of what I'm interested in seeing is how we all differently—
MILA	Okay okay, I get it. Blah blah blah. Gawd.
CAMERON	Ha ha ha ha!
CASSIDY	Whatever. *(to MILA)* Like you don't run your mouth.
CAMERON	Cass, you're only quiet when you're sleeping. Not even.
CASSIDY	Did I ask you what you thought, Blue Boy? Nice package, by the way.
CAMERON	Want some? I'll give you some.
MILA	Can we start please?
CASSIDY	Start then! You're the doctor!

DR. SHEILA/MILA

All right, let's go. Good afternoon, everyone. And welcome to "Tuesday Night Group Therapy." My name is Dr. Sheila and I'll be your therapist. I guess we can start by having you introduce yourselves. Tell me your name and one of your hobbies.

SUNRISE

Hi, Dr. Sheila. I'm Sunrise. I like reading, baking, riding my bike, visiting art galleries...

BLUE BOY

She said one of your hobbies.

SUNRISE

Whatever.

BLUE BOY

My turn. Hi, Sheila. I'm Blue Boy. *(belches loudly)* And I like long, romantic walks on the beach. *(belches again)*

DR. SHEILA/MILA

It's Dr. Sheila. And thank you. Pleasure to meet you both.

BLUE BOY

Pleasure's all mine, Doc.

DR. SHEILA/MILA

So. I'd like to begin by asking what brought you here today. How about we begin with you, Blue Boy? Would you mind sharing with the group what you hope to get out of group therapy? Tell us what your issues are.

BLUE BOY

You tell me. You're the doctor.

DR. SHEILA/MILA

Exactly. I am the doctor. So you have to do what I say.

BLUE BOY

Oooh, doctor. I'm so scared.

DR. SHEILA/MILA

All right, then. Sunrise, would you like to tell me what brought you to therapy?

SUNRISE is silent.

Sunrise?

SUNRISE   I'm thinking. Um.

CAMERON   Well, this is a first.

DR. SHEILA/MILA
            What are your issues, Sunrise?

BLUE BOY   What aren't her issues?

SUNRISE   Whatever, Blue Boy. Why don't you tell Dr. Sheila about your issues?

BLUE BOY   I don't have any issues.

SUNRISE   Ha! Whatever, Michael Jackson.

            Two words: Nose. Jo—

            BLUE BOY cups SUNRISE's mouth to silence her. She bites his hand.

BLUE BOY   Ow! Fuck you, I hate you!

SUNRISE   No you don't, you love me.

            BLUE BOY is silent.

            You love me.

BLUE BOY   Come here. I do love you.

SUNRISE   Stop it, Cameron—I mean, Blue Boy! It always has to get dirty with you.

BLUE BOY	Oh, shush. As if you don't like it.
SUNRISE	Can you not behave normally for, like, five minutes.
BLUE BOY	What's normal, Sunrise?
SUNRISE	Normal is normal.
BLUE BOY	No, normal is if it's on your terms. Otherwise it's "dirty."
SUNRISE	Whatever.
BLUE BOY	"Whatever," yeah. You're doing it now. It's all about control with you.
SUNRISE	Look who's talking. What the hell do you know?
DR. SHEILA/MILA	Be quiet the both of you! Neither of you will benefit from this session if you don't co-operate.
	Blue Boy, I want you tell me why you're here. Now.
BLUE BOY	*(mocking)* I want you to tell me why you're here. Now!

> *Picks up a scarf and wraps it around his neck, as if a woman/* DR. SHEILA.

I'm the doctor, I think I'm sooo smart.

SUNRISE	What is your problem?
BLUE BOY	*(takes lighter from a table and starts flicking it on and off)* You wanna know why I'm here?

You wanna know why I'm here, huh?

I'm here to start a fire! *(pretends to light edge of scarf with lighter)*

DR. SHEILA/MILA

        (grabs lighter from BLUE BOY, *holds it to his chin)* Tell me why you're here, Blue Boy! Why'd you come to Dr. Sheila's Tuesday Night Group Therapy, huh? Tell me, you little shit!

CASSIDY   Okay, guys. Okay okay okay. Pause for a sec. Please. Be careful, all right. Just, you know, be gentle with each other. How about we try some hypnotherapy?

BLUE BOY   I wanna hynotize you, Sunrise.

SUNRISE   Oh Lord.

BLUE BOY   Baby, I'm gonna get you to do whatever I want.

SUNRISE   No, you won't. She's the doctor. Dr. Sheila, you're gonna hypnotize us, right?

BLUE BOY   Oh please, you know you want this.

DR. SHEILA/MILA

        Actually, Sunrise will go first. Sunrise, you hypnotize Blue Boy.

SUNRISE   Ha, in your face! Okay, sit down, Blue Boy. Close your legs! All right. Do you see this set of keys? I want you to follow it with your eyes.

        Don't look at me! Look at the keys!

BLUE BOY   I'm looking, I'm looking!

SUNRISE   You are getting sleepy. So very sleepy. Your eyelids feel fat, heavy. They weigh fifteen pounds each. They're oh so heavy…

BLUE BOY   I'm sleepy. I get it.

SUNRISE	When I count to five and snap my fingers, you'll wake up. And every single time you hear me say the word "cereal," you are going to bray like a donkey. All right? Here we go:
	One. Two. Three. Four. Five. *(snap)*
BLUE BOY	Oh look, I'm awake. Though I feel as if I've just come out of a deep, trance-like sleep. Wonder how that happened?
SUNRISE	Wow, I'm so hungry. I haven't had anything to eat today except a bowl of ce-re-al.
BLUE BOY	Hee-haw. Hee-haw. Hee-haw.
	All right, now it's my turn. See this here set of keys, my little Sunshine?
SUNRISE	Sunrise. Not Sunshine. Sunrise.
BLUE BOY	Fine: Sunrise. Do you or do you not see these keys?
SUNRISE	Yes, I do. They're quite lovely, actually. They—
BLUE BOY	Shhhht. Quiet.
	Follow the keys. Follow the keys with your eyes. Ah hah! Good girl. On the count of three, you'll fall instantly into a deep sleep. When I snap my fingers you'll wake up, and you will do exactly, exactly as I tell you. Do you understand?
SUNRISE	Yes.
BLUE BOY	Okay, here we go: One. Two. Three.
	Snap.
	Sunrise. I'd like for you to touch yourself.

SUNRISE	No.
BLUE BOY	Uh uh, Sunshine. This is Tuesday Night Group Therapy and right now you're hypnotized. You'll do as I say, willingly, because you're in a state of heightened suggestibility. Touch yourself.

SUNRISE touches her nose.

BLUE BOY	That's not what I meant. You know what I meant, Sunshine.
SUNRISE	Dr. Sheila! Hello! Aren't you supposed to be supervising us?
DR. SHEILA/MILA	You guys seem to be doing just fine on your own.
SUNRISE	But you're the therapist. Don't you want to interpret and guide us?
DR. SHEILA/MILA	Forget it—you guys don't listen. Dr. Sheila's tired, all right? Dr. Sheila has laundry that needs to get done.
CASSIDY	Fine then, we'll switch. You be Dr. Sheila then, Blue Boy. And Mila, you're a patient now—Rosa.
MILA	Huh?
CASSIDY	Rosa. That's your character's name, remember?
	Hey, are you mad at me?
MILA	No, I'm just tired. A bit grumpy.
CASSIDY	You sure?
MILA	Yeah. No, really. I'm kind of exhausted actually.

CASSIDY   Okay, well this shouldn't go that much longer. It's helping me.
           It really is. Let me just see Cameron play doctor, okay? But
           yeah, let's get going. Yoo whooo! Dr. Sheila!

DR. SHEILA/CAMERON
           Yes, hello?

SUNRISE   Well, are we gonna start?

DR. SHEILA/CAMERON
           Well, are you gonna sit on that chair?

                SUNRISE sits.

           You too, hot stuff. Asseois-toi.

ROSA   I'm good leaning here. I don't wanna sit.

DR. SHEILA/CAMERON
           Rosa, sit down please. I have an exercise I'd like to try and you
           should both be seated for it.

ROSA   No. I'm good here. My back hurts. I don't want to sit, okay?
           We can do it with me standing.

DR. SHEILA/CAMERON
           Actually, we can't. Which is why I asked you to take a seat.

SUNRISE   Just sit already! Gosh.

ROSA   No, I don't want to. Don't tell me what to do.

SUNRISE   I don't see what the big deal is—you can't just sit so we can
           start this?

ROSA   He tells you to sit, you sit. You fucking do anything he says.
           You're such a baby.

SUNRISE   I'm a baby? Well, you're completely unreasonable. Everything
           has to go precisely your way.

ROSA   So? Better than being a baby.

SUNRISE   I just want to do the scene. But noooo! We can't. Because Miss
           Thing over here is too good to take a seat. This is bullcrap.

DR. SHEILA/CAMERON
           Did you just say "bullcrap"? You are a baby—shut up.

ROSA   Tell me about it.

SUNRISE   *(to DR. SHEILA)* Whatever! I'm on your side!

DR. SHEILA/CAMERON
           Who says I need you on my side? Rosa, are you gonna sit
           down or what?

           DR. SHEILA/CAMERON and ROSA are silent for a moment.

ROSA   Dr. Sheila, go fuck yourself.

SUNRISE   Whoa! Somebody needs to take a chill pill.

           Can we do some hypnosis now, Dr. Sheila?

DR. SHEILA/CAMERON
           Sunshine, will you—

SUNRISE   Sunrise. You keep calling me Sunshine.

DR. SHEILA/CAMERON
           Sunshine. Sunrise. Sunray. Who cares? Yeah, we'll do hypnosis.
           I'll hypnotize you and shut you the fuck up!

SUNRISE   Whatever.

ROSA picks up a doll from the table while they're fighting. She sticks it into the front of her dress. It falls all the way through and out of the dress onto the floor. Both she and DR. SHEILA/ CAMERON reach for it but he's faster; he grabs the doll and holds it behind his back.

ROSA   Give it.

DR. SHEILA/CAMERON
              Sure, no problem. I'll give you the doll—

SUNRISE   Her name is Baby.

DR. SHEILA/CAMERON & ROSA
              (in unison) Shut up!

SUNRISE   Whatever.

DR. SHEILA/CAMERON
              I'll give you the doll back when you sit your ass down.

ROSA   Fuck you.

DR. SHEILA/CAMERON
              Fuck your momma.

ROSA   Hey!?

DR. SHEILA/CAMERON
              Hey what?

ROSA   No momma jokes! For the hundredth fucking time!

DR. SHEILA/CAMERON
              Um. Rosa. I believe we—as in I, Dr. Sheila, and you, Rosa—
              have just met... what... ten minutes ago? And seeing as we've
              so recently met, you've never had the opportunity to tell me
              anything about momma jokes.

ROSA   Well, what kind of crackpot therapist tells his clients to "fuck their mommas" in the first place, Dr. Sheila?

DR. SHEILA/CAMERON
    Well, what kind of a client is too much of a stubborn bitch to sit her ass down?

ROSA   Who you calling a "bitch," asshole? And give me that.

    ROSA lunges for the doll again but misses.

DR. SHEILA/CAMERON
    Fine. Take it.

ROSA   Thank you. *(to the doll)* That's right, back to Momma. Much better here with me than with that scary, scary man.

DR. SHEILA/CAMERON
    Yeah, that's right: love that little baby. Funny—didn't imagine you'd be into babies. Seeing as you're not so into pregnancies.

SUNRISE Oh shit.

ROSA   What the fuck is that supposed to mean?

DR. SHEILA/CAMERON
    Nothing.

ROSA   What's he talking about, Sunrise? Huh? What the fuck is he talking about?

SUNRISE Um. I don't. I'm sorry.

DR. SHEILA/CAMERON
    Forget it, all right? Can we just dr—

ROSA   Drop it? No no no. Nuh uh. We're not dropping this. Let's explore this one further, Dr. Sheila.

CAMERON   Mila, please.

ROSA   You're the one that brought it up. I'm "not so into pregnan-
             cies," huh? Now what, pray tell, Dr. Sheila, led you to that
             conclusion?

CAMERON   Mila.

ROSA   I'm sorry. Who's Mila? My name is Rosa and I'm here for
             group motherfucking therapy. You, my therapist, who I've
             known for all of twelve minutes now, have just informed me,
             much to my surprise, that I, Rosa, am not "into pregnancies"?
             I wanna fucking discuss that, Dr. Sheila.

CAMERON   Look, I'm sorry, okay. I'm sorry. I can't believe I said that. Can
             we drop it now. Please.

MILA   Drop it? Like they dropped you at your job? You knifed-up
             loser.

             Get the fuck out of my house!

                 CAMERON *is silent.*

             What? Are you deaf? I said leave!

DR. SHEILA/CAMERON
             This isn't your house, Rosa. This is Dr. Sheila's Tuesday Night
             Group Therapy.

MILA   What? Are you crazy?

DR. SHEILA/CAMERON
             Tell her, Sunrise. Tell her.

MILA   Is he crazy, Cass? Is he? Is he totally nuts?

CASSIDY   Tell her what?

DR. SHEILA/CAMERON

      (yelling) THAT THIS IS GROUP THERAPY!

BEHIND THE SCENES
WITH AISHA SASHA JOHN

Aisha Sasha John carries an impressive academic record. She has a B.A. in African studies and semiotics from the University of Toronto and an M.F.A. in creative writing from York University. She writes plays, poetry, and short stories, and is a teacher of writing at Humber College.

John says she has had too many beautiful opportunities showcasing her work to pick only three. "If anything, I'll say my favourite gig is the daily performance that goes unseen—when I'm in the trance of the work: at my desk, creating, or in the living room, dancing.

Since those in the Playwrights Unit were asked to write a play inspired by a piece of visual art, the painting Aisha chose was called *Group Therapy* by a Canadian artist named Eliza Griffiths. Says John: "Her work is surreal, sexy, and playful. *Group Therapy* in particular shouted at me with its narrative possibility. I responded to the call."

The best thing about writing plays for Aisha is the thrill of seeing them performed. "It's nothing less than magical to experience other artists entering my imagination and making my creation their own."

Great honesty characterizes her definition of the worst thing about writing plays. It is, in her opinion, "actually the flipside of the best thing. Theatre is always collaborative, so in order to see one's idea fully realized, it's necessary to have a bunch of other people involved."

Reaching for a magnum opus, or "hugeness," as she says, is John's next goal. Specifically, a poetry manuscript, *The Shining Material*. She is also working on a full-length play about a girl named Plum. With that, Aisha hopes to create a work that can function both as poetry and theatre. She's interested in the idea of a play where the words themselves are essential, not just as vehicles to advance the story, but where the theatre is in the speech itself.

When asked about Obsidian's contribution to Canadian theatre, Aisha says: "Obsidian has an important role in the theatre community in that it provides points of entry for emerging artists and theatre professionals as well as important opportunities for the more seasoned. It's exciting to know there's a space dedicated to nourishing and sharing Black Canadian voices."

THE COOKIE
BY ROSEMARIE STEWART

voice give just granite company black theatre
OBSIDIAN ENCOURAGEMENT GLASS STRONG JET
SPACE VOICE GIVE JUST GRANITE COMPANY BLACK
THEATRE OBSIDIAN ENCOURAGEMENT GLASS
HARD STRONG SPACE JET VOICE GIVE JUST
GRANITE COMPANY BLACK THEATRE
OBSIDIAN ENCOURAGEMENT GLASS SPAC

CHARACTERS

Mavis: early thirties, slinky nightgown, voluptuous.

Dave: mid-thirties, T-shirt, pyjama pants, slender.

MAVIS and DAVE lie snuggling in bed. The room has a bedside table and lamps on either side of the bed. The room is in semi-darkness. She lies on top of him. They kiss passionately and attempt to have sex.

In the stillness of the room, we hear the sound of munching. MAVIS rolls off DAVE in a huff and flicks on the light.

MAVIS   *(angry)* Every night it's the same damn thing.

DAVE sits up in bed chewing on a cookie.

Dave, what's going on?

DAVE   *(evasive)* Nothing's going on, Mavis.

He continues eating and brushes crumbs off his pyjama top; some crumbs land on her.

MAVIS   Don't brush them on me!

She grabs a corner of the sheet to shake off the crumbs. DAVE continues eating without a word.

What's the matter with you?

MAVIS sweeps her hands over her body, pointing to herself.

Look at me, Dave.

DAVE keeps his head down, busy nibbling on a chocolate chip.

(pleading) Look at me.

    DAVE looks up at her and then quickly turns his attention back to the cookie.

Don't you want me anymore?

    DAVE sighs, wipes crumbs off his face.

DAVE   Can we drop it? I have to get up early tomorrow.

MAVIS   Yeah, that's the only thing that will be up tomorrow.

    She busies herself smoothing the bedspread that covers her lap, visibly annoyed.

DAVE   That's right. Make your snide remarks. That'll make me hot for you. *(mutters)* Like that'll ever happen.

MAVIS   What's that?

DAVE   Nothing.

    MAVIS moves closer to him and begins kissing his neck, moaning in pleasure. She quickly turns off the light and continues kissing his neck.

    The unmistakable sound of munching is heard. She stops kissing him and moves away.

MAVIS   *(irritated)* What are you doing?

DAVE   *(through a mouthful)* Nothing.

MAVIS   *(accusatory)* Why are you doing that?

DAVE   *(chewing loudly)* What?

MAVIS   You know what.

              She flicks the light on, sits up, crosses her arms.

DAVE   I don't know what you're talking about.

MAVIS   *(sighs)* It's not helping, you know.

DAVE   *(defensive)* Do you have to go on about it? It's hard enough
              trying to concentrate as it is.

              MAVIS laughs, sarcastic.

              Yeah, that's right. Laugh it up.

MAVIS   *(harshly)* You know, Dave, you are the biggest pussy I know.
              (imitating his voice) The cookie calms my nerves. I need it.
              (exasperated) God, just once could you be a man and admit
              you've got a problem?!

              *DAVE pulls out an enormous cookie from under the covers, takes
              a big bite and chews defiantly.*

              *MAVIS frowns as she watches DAVE eating. She fluffs her pillow,
              adjusting it behind her back.*

              (quietly) Maybe if you didn't try so hard...

DAVE   I don't want to hear it. You don't get it. I'm under a lot of
              pressure.

              He punctuates each word with a bite of the cookie.

MAVIS   I'm sorry, Dave. It's just so... strange to have to compete
              with... *(gestures at the cookie)* with something like that.

MAVIS slides over to DAVE and tries to wrap his arm around her shoulders. DAVE allows her to move his arm, waits until she's settled and then takes another bite.

(indignant) I can't believe you.

DAVE   *(rolling his eyes)* Here we go.

MAVIS   I can't believe you won't even try without—without that,

DAVE swallows, then says quietly:

DAVE   I need it.

MAVIS   *(seductively)* Honey, you don't need it. All you need is me.

MAVIS kneels on the bed to show off her shapely figure in her silk nightgown. DAVE looks longingly at her and then at the cookie. He licks his lips, considering.

MAVIS sits down very close to him.

Can't we at least try, Dave?

DAVE wipes sweat from his forehead. He still holds the cookie in one hand.

DAVE   All right. All right, Mave. *(exhales loudly)* I can do this.

MAVIS   *(smiles)* I know you can.

DAVE   We've done it before.

She touches his arm, caressing it softly.

MAVIS   Yes we have.

DAVE   *(with a faint smile)* And we can do it again…

He pulls the covers over their heads. They giggle as they writhe around, their bodies in silhouette beneath the sheets.

MAVIS   Oh, honey, I knew you could do it.

DAVE   Just, just stop talking okay?

MAVIS   Okay. I just love you so much. *(pause)* Do you love me?

DAVE   *(with effort)* I can't—you can't— Just be quiet right now.

MAVIS, in silhouette, gets up on one elbow.

MAVIS   What? Now I can't ask you if you love me?

DAVE   *(groans)* No, no, no, no…

MAVIS   You don't love me?

DAVE pulls her back toward him.

DAVE   Just let me…

MAVIS   What do you mean? Do you love me or not?

DAVE   Woman, can you just be quiet?!

MAVIS   Excuse me?!

Munching sounds come from under the blanket. MAVIS flings the covers off and bolts up. She stares at DAVE.

Okay—that's it. I'm leaving and I'm not coming back.

DAVE   Why'd you have to be like that, Mavis?

MAVIS   You know why. Or is there more to this thing than you're letting on?

DAVE   What are you talking about?

                  MAVIS continues speaking as if DAVE isn't there,

MAVIS   I should've seen it. I knew it was suspicious. But oh no, I had
                  to make up another excuse for you.

                  Cookie crumbs fall everywhere, DAVE looks bewildered, watch-
                  ing MAVIS.

DAVE   Huh?

                  MAVIS points an accusing finger at him.

MAVIS   You're trying to kill me, aren't you?

DAVE   What?

                  She continues, certainty making her words spill out faster.

MAVIS   Yeah. I didn't want to see it but now it's clear. You want me dead.

                  DAVE starts to look worried, reaches out to her with chocolate-
                  stained fingers, pleading.

DAVE   Mavis, you're talking crazy. You know I love you.

                  She shrinks to the edge of the bed.

MAVIS   Don't touch me! You cold-hearted murderer.

DAVE   I'm not a murderer. I haven't killed anybody—

MAVIS   *(overlaps)* —Not yet. And I'm not going to give you that chance.

                  Her words sink in. DAVE is incredulous, speaking slowly, search-
                  ing her expression for any indication that she's listening to him.

DAVE	C'mon. You don't really think I'd do a thing like that, do you?

MAVIS, distracted, brushes crumbs off her arm.

MAVIS	I didn't want to. But just look at this place. Everywhere I turn it's there.

DAVE begins sweeping crumbs off the bed with one hand, with the other hand he stuffs the remains of the cookie into his mouth.

DAVE	I'll clean it up. I will.

MAVIS	*(folds her arms)* How long have we known each other?

DAVE	Er...

MAVIS	See? You don't even know. It's been eight years. Eight years! *(tearfully)* And instead of putting a ring on my finger you want to get rid of me.

DAVE	Eight years? *(reaches out to her)* Honey, I'm sorry. Don't cry.

MAVIS	*(shakes his hand off)* That's it. It's either me or that, that thing.

DAVE pulls out another enormous cookie from beside the bed, takes a big bite and rests it on his lap.

DAVE	*(through a mouthful of cookie)* Baby, you know I love you. But this cookie is so good.

MAVIS	That cookie is ruining our lives, Dave! Just look at you. You can't even bear to leave it alone. You take it everywhere.

She reaches into the nightstand, takes out a pack of cigarettes and lighter, puts a cigarette in her mouth, and lights it, inhaling deeply. She blows smoke into the air.

DAVE doesn't seem to notice the smoke, fidgets, chewing slowly, avoiding her eyes.

You get to work late because you just have to have more of your precious cookie. I can't even carry on a decent conversation with you because you're thinking about it... or eating it...

MAVIS rummages in the nightstand, pulls out an ashtray and flicks ash into it before taking another drag.

Sometimes I think you're more in love with it than you are with me.

DAVE   *(munching)* What?

MAVIS gets out of bed, cigarette dangling from her lips, pulls on a bathrobe and turns to face DAVE, taking a drag and exhaling, gesticulating with the cigarette.

MAVIS   Tell me something. Did you think it was funny to lead me on all these years? Killing me bit by bit.

She paces beside the bed. DAVE motions with the cookie as he speaks.

DAVE   Lead you on? Just because a man wants to have a snack, now I'm leading you on?

A piece of the cookie breaks off and lands on her pillow. MAVIS stops in her tracks, looks at it in disgust.

MAVIS   *(angrily)* I can't take this anymore. You and your cookie and your crumbs.

She blows smoke at him and stubs out the cigarette angrily before turning to pace again.

DAVE is becoming agitated, shoving hunks of cookie into his mouth, pulling his hair, breathing hard.

DAVE

(munching) You never listen!

He cradles the remains of the cookie defensively.

MAVIS

Dave, take a good look at yourself. Just look at what you've become. You're disturbed, David. There's something wrong with you.

She leans in, trying to make eye contact with him.

Why won't you talk to me?

DAVE shifts in his seat, suddenly aware of the smoke for the first time. He waves one hand to clear the air, still grasping a piece of cookie in his other hand.

DAVE

I thought you quit smoking.

MAVIS stubs the cigarette out in the ashtray, defiant, then lights another, blowing smoke into the air.

MAVIS

(casually) I did… when you promised to give up your cookie thing.

DAVE

I trusted you. You said you'd quit.

MAVIS

Yeah, when you said you'd quit. So now we're even, right?

She inhales deeply, exhaling while looking at DAVE, then sits on the edge of the bed, crosses her legs, swinging one as she speaks.

Well, I guess I lied. Just like you. Doesn't that just make you crazy?

DAVE	*(coughs slightly)* C'mon Mavis. You're not being fair. This is your health we're talking about. And mine.
MAVIS	Oh you are not going to turn this around on me.

She picks up a box of cookies wedged between the bed and the wall, waves it at him.

The issue is your emotional obsession.

He sits silently. After a moment:

DAVE	Well at least I don't smoke them.

MAVIS tosses the box onto the nightstand.

MAVIS	Uhh...! I can't deal with you.

She butts out the cigarette and lights another, pacing around again.

A cellphone rings on the bedside table. MAVIS picks it up.

(speaking into the phone) Hello?

Listens a moment.

I can't talk right now.

DAVE moves closer to MAVIS, trying to overhear. MAVIS turns her back to him, speaks quietly into the phone.

No... I told you... okay... maybe... Let's talk tomorrow.

She hangs up the phone, places it back on the nightstand. A brief silence.

DAVE	Who was that?

MAVIS   It was Joe.

DAVE   That's great. Just great.

He fidgets with a piece of cookie.

So how long have you been talking to your ex-boyfriend?

MAVIS   Oh relax. It's nothing.

DAVE   It's always nothing when it's you and your issues.

MAVIS   Everything would be better between us if you would just let it go—

The doorbell rings. MAVIS *turns toward the door, exits.*

(offstage) Who could that be?

The sound of a door opening.

(offstage) Yes?

MAN'S VOICE   *(offstage)* Delivery for you. If you could sign here, ma'am.

The sound of a door closing. MAVIS *returns to the bedroom and stands in the doorway holding a box wrapped in brown paper.*

DAVE *perks up at the sight of the box, scrambles to get to it; he hurries off the bed, his foot getting tangled in the sheets, falling hard to the floor.*

The dislodged sheet reveals stacks of cookie boxes under the bed.

MAVIS   Dave!

She rushes to his side, putting the box down while she bends over him. DAVE *is prone, moaning weakly.*

Oh my God, Dave! Are you all right?

> *MAVIS touches his forehead, gingerly, fearful.*

David! Can you hear me?

> *DAVE mumbles, his eyes opening, looking beyond MAVIS at the brown package on the floor. She leans closer to him.*

What is it? Speak to me.

> *DAVE reaches toward her, then his hand falls onto the box; he tries to open the wrapping with two fingers.*

DAVE   Chocolate praline.

> *MAVIS shoves him aside, gets up, angry.*

MAVIS   You're pathetic.

> *DAVE sits up, pulls the box closer, tears the paper off, opens it, then eats a cookie with gusto. He takes his cookie box to bed and gets comfortable.*

> *MAVIS turns to leave the room and stubs her toe on a book lying on the floor.*

Oww!

> *She stands on one foot, rubbing her injured toe, then crouches down to look closer at the book. She picks it up.*

What is this?! *(reads the title out loud) 101 Cookie Recipes?*

> *MAVIS stands up.*

So now you've got a cookie recipe book? I am so sick of this, Dave.

She flings the book across the room, narrowly missing DAVE's head. The book bangs against the wall and falls to the floor.

DAVE   You're sick of this? *(laughs sardonically)* You're sick of this? *(leans toward her)* Do you know what it's like living with you?

He gets on all fours in the bed, becoming crazed as he speaks. MAVIS holds the lapels of her bathrobe closed with one hand, looking nervously at DAVE.

MAVIS   *(dismissively)* What are you talking about?

DAVE   Shut up! Just shut up!

MAVIS recoils, standing fixed on the spot. DAVE sits cross-legged on the bed.

(counting on his fingers) You're judgmental, you're mean, you treat me like I'm not the man in this relationship.

He flails his arms around, his voice raising.

(brandishing the cookie) I get more from this cookie than I've ever gotten from you. You want to know why we're not married? We're not married because I can't stand being with you!

He gestures wildly while he speaks.

Why would I want to be with someone like you when you never let me be me. You never let me be the man, Mavis. *(pounds his chest)* I'm the man! *(confidently)* And when I eat my cookie, I'm in control. I'm the boss. I eat it when I want to eat it, how I want to eat it. *(takes a bite)* And it tastes sweeter than you, too.

He pauses a moment, savouring the taste of the cookie. MAVIS stands transfixed in the middle of the room.

(resigned) It's not always telling me what I do wrong, how I've failed. I don't want to be with you, Mavis. I never wanted to marry you. It was supposed to be a bit of fun. And the next thing I know you're moved in here, changing everything and hounding me for a ring. Telling me that I love you. And I began to believe it.

MAVIS   (confused) What are you talking about?

DAVE   (speaks as if she hasn't spoken) Or maybe you're the cookie. And every bite I take is one bite closer to freedom.

>   MAVIS backs away fearfully.

(chuckling to himself) Yeah, maybe all it takes to make you disappear is to keep on chewing.

>   He bites off another mouthful and chews, looking pleased with himself.

MAVIS   (voice breaking nervously) You've totally lost your mind, Dave.

DAVE   Good. 'Cause I'm done.

>   MAVIS backs toward the door, watching DAVE closely, then hurriedly rushes out.

>   DAVE sits in bed looking at the closed door then looks lovingly at the cookie resting in his hand. He straightens the covers, settles himself against the pillows and turns off the light.

>   End of scene.

BEHIND THE SCENES
WITH ROSEMARIE STEWART

Rosemarie Stewart, in addition to being a playwright, is a technical, science, and policy writer with many years of experience. She increasingly wishes that she could leave non-fiction writing so audiences may enjoy her skills in the theatre and media.

Being a storyteller is Stewart's favourite self-definition. She is a writer for stage, film, and television, while continuing her family's vibrant oral history. A cherished credit is working as a Juno-nominated singer, touring Canada and Europe in a band. Rosemarie comments that this is a great way to see Canada and explore several countries overseas. With everything Stewart works on, she draws upon her background as a British-born woman of Jamaican heritage.

The Cookie was inspired by a women's fitness group that Stewart was running as a personal trainer. Many of her clients struggled with food cravings and sweet temptations. It was a running joke in the class that the women would blame cookies for their lack of motivation or as an excuse to have an easier workout. "Having a hard time doing those crunches? Blame the cookies. Want a longer break between sets? Blame the cookies. It stuck. I expanded on that idea as a way to explore intimacy issues between a couple."

The best thing about writing plays, states Rosemarie, is that you can create your own world or peek into other worlds. She believes the writer is the omniscient presence who has the power to get inside characters' heads, travel the globe, and have experiences ranging from the incredible to the mundane. Stewart quips that she can fall in love, or have characters and situations that she loves to hate, with just about anything she creates. And to top it all off, she can share that love with audiences.

Rosemarie Stewart's bad news about playwriting is "the solitary confinement you have to enter to move from concept to completion. It's a lonely road sometimes on the journey of creativity. No one can really be part of it because you are always on the line. Let's face it, it's your baby; and you're the only one who has that bond with it."

Stewart views the best and worst aspects of playwriting as circular, saying, "once you've completed your fledgling play, you have to be ready to face other people's opinions. But that leads to the best thing about writing plays: you, the playwright, can have the satisfaction of knowing that you created something that only you could do."

Next on the agenda for Rosemarie is producing her first independent feature film. Another goal is a stage production of one of Stewart's full-length plays. She is grateful for the opportunity Obsidian has given her to have her voice heard on the Canadian stage.

Rosemarie Stewart wants to leave us and herself laughing: "I'm a Brit. I have a different sense of humour—dry humour combined with the absolutely hilarious stories gathered from my family's Jamaican storytelling heritage. It's so much fun. Laughter and I are well-acquainted. It's generational."

SOCIAL ISSUES
TOO TOUGH TO IGNORE

Exit Velocity
By Rita Shelton Deverell

voice give just granite company black theatre
OBSIDIAN ENCOURAGEMENT GLASS STRONG JET
SPACE VOICE GIVE JUST GRANITE COMPANY BLACK
THEATRE OBSIDIAN ENCOURAGEMENT GLASS
HARD STRONG SPACE JET VOICE GIVE JUST
GRANITE COMPANY BLACK THEATRE
OBSIDIAN ENCOURAGEMENT GLASS SPAC

CHARACTERS

He: Saul, a very elderly gentleman.

She: Misty, a youngish woman.

Staging—if staged: The paintings of waves become a seemingly endless series of screens from which the actors can emerge, do the three scenes in front of or behind or both.

SCENE I...

Scene i... is in an airplane. A luxury double seat faces the beautiful waves. Muzak by Vivaldi plays.

HE   First class.

SHE   Way to go.

HE   Are you frightened?

SHE   *(taking a flute glass from a tray)* Champagne to calm me. Who can ask for more. "If I've got the luxuries, why worry about the necessities." Somebody said that didn't they?

HE   Frank Lloyd Wright. Or was it Oscar Wilde? That statement is also sometimes attributed to Brother Langston Hughes.

SHE   *(giggles)* That's three somebodies.

HE   Ah, champagne. There is a justification. The queen mother lived to be well over one hundred by drinking a glass a day, if memory serves.

SHE	But you can't beat this beautiful cabin, gorgeous artwork. Relaxing cyber-art. It's like those fire logs people watched for hours in Vancouver.
	That seemed stupid at the time.
	Now— Relax... relax... breathe in...
HE	Please don't forget to breathe out.
SHE	I am a little scared. I guess it shows. I'm chattering away. Maybe we're going to die.
HE	We definitely are. That, at least, is not a matter of supposition.
SHE	Okay. Okay. But not in this plane I hope.
	I'm Misty. Misty Dawn.
	Are you one of those old jazz players?
HE	What?
MISTY	Well I heard that they've almost brought Preservation Hall back. And the French Quarter.
	And you're kind of brown...
HE	*(laughs)* And truly old...
	Am I well-preserved?
	I am afraid there is not a musical bone in this old body. Although I did, on a trip long ago with my late beloved wife of fifty-five years, go to Preservation Hall.
MISTY	I'm sorry... I just figured maybe... with your being a distinguished, brown older gentleman...

I didn't mean it quite that way. I just thought you might be helping with the jazz revival.

HE   Well I *am* going to help. I hope.

          I am Saul.

MISTY   *(puzzled, not harsh)* Saul what?

SAUL   I do have a first name, but everybody just calls me Saul. My mother could not resist a first name of "Ami," for friend. So, I'm Ami Saul.

MISTY   My friend Saul? …Mr. Saul…

SAUL   Just call me Saul.

          And what takes you to the Big Easy, Ms. Dawn?

MISTY   Just call me Misty. I'm going to a really important big-ticket TV and film convention. It's my first really big chance.

SAUL   I don't think I know anything about that area of human endeavour. But congratulations nevertheless.

          What we hope for, and work for, we should get at least a little bit of.

MISTY   I really don't like flying though. My boss paid for everything, first class, and said meet him there.

SAUL   He must think very highly of you.

MISTY   I'm crossing my fingers. That he thinks highly of me. My first chance to prove myself. At the Big Meeting.

          I intend to make myself an indispensable member of the company.

How are you going to help?

SAUL   I will disinfect houses I've been told. And paint. Do electrical
        work. And plumbing. I am pretty good at that. I will not do
        the drywall. Plaster dust is bad for my lungs at this stage.

MISTY   Are you serious?

SAUL   I am only worried about carrying the tools by myself. They
        are heavy.

        And I don't much like heat, although I have travelled to many
        hot places. In every sense.

        And I hope they will not think I am a terrorist. Don't you
        think I look too old to be a terrorist?

MISTY   But Mr. Saul. That hurricane was three years ago. Everything
        is rebuilt.

SAUL   Not quite. You will see, Ms. Dawn, when you get there. Life is
        none too easy in the Big Easy. Even three years later.

        And as for my fears, the young people on my team say they
        will have a dolly for me and my tools. And when the dolly is
        not available they will carry them.

MISTY   Are you sure about this?

SAUL   Yes. I have never had such certainty.

        I am not sure about flying first class though! It is absurd. It
        seems an odd way to travel to assist homeless people.

        But my children will not let me fly unless I have easy access to
        oxygen. And unless I can stretch my legs out so I do not arrive
        at my destination all cramped up.

Not to New Orleans—not to Afghanistan. Not to Malaysia. Not anywhere. I must fly first class they say. Children are very cautious.

Whereas, at my age, I am taking a risk by putting one foot, then another, over the edge of the bed in the morning. So what is there to be cautious about?

MISTY   Are you sure about this?

SAUL   Not to pry, Ms. Dawn, but are you sure about this man who is paying your way? First class.

MISTY   Call me Misty, Mr. Saul.

SAUL   All right, Ms. Misty.

MISTY   Of course I'm absolutely right about Mr. Right. He is my big-ticket catch.

SAUL   What do you mean? This is new slang to me.

MISTY   Well, he has great connections. I don't have really any. He can write my ticket in the TV business. Make all the contacts.

I've been on the lookout for a meal ticket like this for some time. And I don't mean food…

SAUL   (smiles) I'm getting lost in all these tickets.

I suppose I was asking if you are sure you are safe with this person. Does this person have your best interests at heart.

Could you not write whatever ticket you wish to write yourself, Ms. Dawn?

MISTY   No. It doesn't work that way. I've thought this through.

Mr. Saul, I'm smart. I'm probably even talented. I'm a hard worker, but I've got no connections. None of my family has ever worked in television or film.

After two years of proactive indispensableness—listen to me!—I sound like the business pages in the *Globe and Mail*. Did I just read that in the departure lounge?

Anyway, after two years I'll stand on my own two feet.

It's who you know, not what you know… unfortunately.

SAUL   I have heard that said.

MISTY   I think he doesn't want his wife to know. That's why we're on different planes on different days. She was taking him to the airport.

He'll meet me I think. Although I gave her an amaryllis as a gift so she wouldn't be suspicious.

SAUL   I am sorry, I'm not familiar with this gift.

MISTY   *(giggles)* One of those gorgeous red lilies that are very trendy, very in this time of year. Perfect taste.

SAUL   Oh. Would that be a huge flower with a furry thing that looks like a black widow spider in the centre?

MISTY   Trust me. She'll like it.

It's a signal to her that I'm not interested in his well-toned body, or centre-hallway home, or swimming pool.

I'm only interested in his intellect and my route to a corner office. He can keep his corner office.

SAUL   I think I see *(He doesn't.)*

But there are two sides to every marriage. And perhaps what worries the wife is not so much *your* intentions, but Mr. Right's intentions, Ms. Dawn.

MISTY   Maybe. But this is the perfect gift for perfect reassurance.

SAUL   I know we have just met, although a conversation of three hours is a long time.

>   *Pause.*

If for any reason you wish to telephone me after you are settled in New Orleans, at the Big TV Meeting, please do not hesitate.

MISTY   *(puzzled)* That's kind, Mr. Saul.

SAUL   Just call me Saul. Mr. Right's wife may believe there is a black widow spider jumping out at her.

SCENE II..

>   *A dirty street, city noises, shrieking voices, anger sounds, construction buzz, discordant jazz.* MISTY *frantically looks around.*

SAUL   *(calling from behind a barrier of construction tools)* I am over here! Just one moment please.

MISTY   *(threatented, disoriented, doesn't recognize* SAUL's *voice)* Yeah right. I'm going to wait here.

SAUL   Please don't leave. You've just gotten here.

MISTY   *(moving away from the voice, looks in a different direction)* Uh huh huh. No. No. Back off. Don't touch me, mister.

>   *(shifting her gaze again)* I can stare as much as I want! You're not the only person on this road!

(as if she's under attack) I can gawk. Just try and stop me. It's a free country. I'm free to stare…

SAUL   *(getting very near her)* Misty! Misty!

It's me, Saul.

MISTY   Yeah, just like the Bible. *(almost hysterical)* I just thought of that one…

(returns gaze to SAUL, uncertainly) …Mr. Saul?

SAUL   At your service, gracious lady.

You telephoned.

Just like I asked you to. Thank you.

MISTY   Sorry, you scared me. This place scares me.

I almost turned around on this road and ran back.

Not much has been rebuilt from three years ago, has it… just like you said.

SAUL   But how are *you*, Ms. Misty?

MISTY   Any place we can talk privately? Like a coffee shop or something.

SAUL   Look around.

MISTY   All these desperate people scare me. I thought you were one of them.

SAUL   I am I suppose.

As I did not know exactly when you would get here today, I promised some folks a hand.

MISTY	A hand with what?
SAUL	Their cleanup. Remember, that is why I am here.
	First, I paint the X's off the doors. Then, do the yardwork, carpentry, electrical, plumbing, et cetera.
MISTY	The X's…?
SAUL	Look. Somebody died in that house. Death has signed his name.
MISTY	Can we get out of here? Please?
SAUL	Have you got a few hours before you have to go back uptown to Mr. Right Connections?
MISTY	That's what I want to talk with you about.
	Getting back home.
	I can wait until you're finished your work.
SAUL	No place to wait. You'll have to help.
	Have a paint can.

Hands her one of two two-gallon cans he is carrying while he pulls a dolly with garden tools, carpentry, electrical, plumbing tools, etc.

MISTY	You've been carrying this? You're an old man.
SAUL	And you are a young woman and will make the load so much lighter.
	I can carry the garden tools without too much trouble.
	Actually, it's a miracle. I have hardly been tired at all.

MISTY   Are you saying that just for my benefit? *(tries to smile)*

             I'd like to believe in miracles.

SAUL   You, on the other hand, are looking just a bit fatigued, if I
             may make so unflattering an observation.

             It's very hard to judge who, and what, one can walk out on.
             Do you need me most, Ms. Misty? Or do my children at
             home, who are twice your age, need me more.

             Or these weeds...

MISTY   Raking and weed-pulling—why?

             If they can't live in their houses why worry about the yards?

SAUL   Because the government will charge them $500 to clean up
             the yards and then declare the houses unlivable if someone is
             not occupying them.

MISTY   But they *are* unlivable.

SAUL   No, the people can live here. They want to live here if we
             clean up just a bit.

             You do not need to talk to me about going back uptown
             if you choose to. You don't owe me any explanations, Ms.
             Dawn.

MISTY   That's not what I mean by going home.

SAUL   We can do six yards in the next three hours and then you can
             tell me your problem. Later tonight.

             We can do twelve tomorrow. Twelve yards the next day.

That means I have met my promise to at least one part of humanity. I will have been here for the full week I committed to these people.

Then home as you say.

Although my list says there are also a couple of doors that need hanging. With your help it will all be accomplished.

MISTY   Mr. Saul, you know how to hang a door?

SAUL   Not exactly. Not all that well. But a great deal better than the officially approved construction companies who charge $400 and the doors still do not lock.

MISTY   I guess you're my main chance. Can I be with you another two days?

SAUL   Of course, fair lady.

We will stay in a house where I have personally fixed the door, for some people almost as elderly as I who were afraid to sleep at night. And afraid to leave for even a carton of milk.

My family thinks I should come home and look after them. Right now. Quick, pronto, instantly. And they're very capable of getting their own milk.

Now these people will not get thrown out of their house, the only place they have to live, before they get their insurance.

MISTY   Two someones died in this house?

SAUL   That is right. You're learning to read the death code.

MISTY   I mean, I saw it on the news. People dying in attics. And on rooftops. I guess I didn't really believe it.

SAUL	Believe it.
MISTY	Or that the signs are still here.
SAUL	Right here.
MISTY	Spooky.
SAUL	Not spooky.
	Infuriating. Grief-making. Not acceptable. Unacceptable.
	But not spooky.
	Paint away, Ms. Dawn.
MISTY	*(She paints over two X's.)* This doesn't take away their problem.
SAUL	Oh yes it does.
	Without the X they can walk through the door. They can live a bit better with their reality, which is chronic depression.
MISTY	Like depression where you see a shrink…?
SAUL	Painting the X's and cleaning the yards is a lot cheaper.
	You are doing a good job, Ms. Dawn.
MISTY	And you're not tired? I'm beat already. Two more days of this and I will collapse.
SAUL	*(unlocking his new door)* Ah. Our newly repaired, safe house.
MISTY	And a big, pretty wicker hamper addressed to "Mr. Saul and Friend."
SAUL	I think that must be you, Ms. Misty.

MISTY	*(reads note)* "Dear Lady. Sorry I yelled at you. If you're a friend of Mr. Saul's of course you're here to help—not just to stare at us and take photos when all our walls have tumbled down.
	Please accept my apologies for yelling and enjoy this fried chicken. The menu will be different tomorrow night. Catch you then."
SAUL	Three years ago he was a great chef in the French Quarter. Now he's trying to help the helpers.
MISTY	But where does he cook?
SAUL	In his home, where else? Where we painted out the X's, cleaned the yard, hooked up the electricity, and did not charge him—after all his money was taken, stolen really, by the so-called construction crews.
MISTY	I had to leave him, Saul.
	For at least a half-hour I was so angry I thought I'm getting this XYZ-SOB out of my life. These boots are made for walking... all the way downtown.
	But now I'm out of steam. Got no money, no air ticket, no room.
SAUL	In the big fancy hotel? Where the big fancy meeting is?
MISTY	Yes, I guess I'm homeless and abandoned.
SAUL	Why did you leave him?
MISTY	I can't remember anymore.
SAUL	Yes you can. What did he do?
MISTY	He picked away at me. I felt six inches tall. Said I was too ambitious. Too pushy. Too ambitious without real talent.

Too aggressive without a real brain. That I'd sink without him. I was just using him.

I should just stop pushing in the middle of his every conversation, every meeting, every deal. Butting in when I wasn't giving anything.

That I wasn't putting out enough. Would I never get it? That I was on the take. That putting out was all he needed me here for.

SAUL   Putting out enough…

MISTY   …Exactly.

Can you get me back to Canada?

SAUL   Of course. If that is what you want.

After the telephone calls I've gotten today, I suppose I really do have to go back. But I will not break faith with these people and leave early just to rush back to my very grown-up children. Let them cry on each other's shoulders. They should start to practise now for when my shoulder is gone.

And you are not homeless, Ms. Dawn, nor abandoned. Nor is my daughter alone.

These people were abandoned. On their roofs. No last rites or words. Alone.

MISTY   I feel like I've been left to die.

Maybe I am condemned to be alone all my life. And my big break will never come. Maybe I don't deserve it.

SAUL   Ms. Misty, one is always ultimately alone. But you have made an adult, mature decision. It hasn't been snatched from you. You will make your own big break.

MISTY   Couldn't we just check into a safe hotel uptown?

We could be killed here. We could be robbed.

SAUL   No, because we hung a door that locks properly for our friends here.

And the whole neighbourhood knows we are here—not staring at their misery, but helping.

How safe has it been for you?

MISTY   Don't lecture me, please. I feel badly enough as it is.

Let's just leave it that I've made some really bad choices. That sounds pretty effing respectable, doesn't it?

Well Mom, Dad, Sis, Grandma, Girlfriend, Mr. Saul—I've made some really bad choices. Babble babble babble.

SAUL   No lectures. No apologies required. *(almost thundering)* Maybe I will be alone all my life too, after telling my children I will not come home because they ordered me to.

They have always tried to tell me what to do. But this is the first time I've not listened to their directives. Maybe it will break our relationship.

MISTY   Mr. Saul, didn't you just tell me we are all alone. At least *you* made your decision.

We will not backpedal on our own decisions and break faith with ourselves.

SAUL   My family worries about me 24/7, they say, when I go to these trouble spots.

Hurts them more than it hurts me, they say. I say, we are all going to die anyway, Ms. Dawn.

But not in this disinfected house. After all, I cleaned it myself.

MISTY   You think.

SAUL   I think you have had a lot more garbage in your life than this.

Sweep it in the bin.

SCENE III.

On an airplane as in Scene i.

MISTY   First class.

SAUL   Frightened?

MISTY   Champagne to calm me.

SAUL   Well I suppose that helps. The queen mother lived to be over one hundred and she drank a glass a day.

MISTY   Saul, how old are you anyway?

SAUL   Approaching ninety. Very fast.

MISTY   You could have died in New Orleans.

SAUL   I am going to die anyway. Given my age it probably will be sooner rather than later.

Your spirit was almost murdered on the other hand.

MISTY   Don't rub it in.

I said I've made some terrible choices.

But I've still got my brain. And my ambition. And my creativity... And you've found a bit of compassion in me.

SAUL   More than just a tiny pinch, Ms. Misty.

MISTY   I'll be able to pay you back as soon as I get access to my bank accounts again.

Some of those people last night, those Black people, not that I mind them being Black...

SAUL   Of course you don't...

MISTY   But they weren't even grateful to you for what you'd done.

SAUL   How do you know that?

They didn't try to kill our brains, or ambitions, or spirits, on the other hand.

And some were able to say thank you. Like our friend the former chef who made all the food for that lovely goodbye party.

MISTY   I'd like to say thank you by paying your money back.

And do something really nice.

SAUL   Ms. Dawn, can I ask you to do me a huge favour?

MISTY   Anything.

SAUL   Please come to the hospital with me. As soon as we get to Toronto.

MISTY   But you said you were feeling fine, not even tired.

SAUL	I am.
	But my daughter is not. She is dying.
MISTY	What?
SAUL	I got the call right after I got yours, saying you were coming down to meet me in the Lower Ninth Ward.
	Critically ill the hospital said.
MISTY	And you stayed for two days to clean up yards and paint out X's.
SAUL	My daughter will leave this life anyway. Whether I rush to her bedside or not.
	So will I. So will you.
	I have prayed to the Creator to hold her for me until I get to say goodbye. Other people who love her are with her now.
MISTY	But you are not.
SAUL	No. And I also fervently pray that I have done at least as much of the right thing as I can. I decided to stay with people who had no one beside them—at all.
	And if I am wrong, I will have to live with that. And die with that.
MISTY	I would have made you go back right away if you had told me.
SAUL	I know. That, gracious lady, is most probably why I did not tell you.
	I would not have *made* you do anything, I hope. You are grown up now, Ms. Misty. You can write your own ticket.

But I am afraid to go alone. I'm not afraid of my daughter. But of her partner, and her in-laws, and my grandchildren. What will they think of me…

I am humbly asking you to accompany me. At least my daughter is not in her attic alone. Whether we get there in time, or whether we do not.

MISTY   When it's all over, can I invite you and your family to my grandma's cottage?

Gran's younger than you are. That seems amazing.

We'll wait on you hand and foot.

SAUL   Will anything ever really be all over?

      Tries to twinkle.

Are you trying to be a matchmaker for me, Ms. Dawn.

MISTY   I wouldn't dream of it. I'm just trying to be with you and not embarrass myself.

SAUL   You will do that by taking me to the hospital. And you are not embarrassing in the least.

Thank you, gracious lady. The visit sounds nice.

First-class service in a luxury cottage.

MISTY   So you'll come.

SAUL   Oh, I don't know.

When it's all over, with my daughter that is, I think I had better go back down to New Orleans, where I can be of some real use.

MISTY	No, you'll come with me.
	I can write my own ticket now. And yours too.
	You just said so.
SAUL	I beg your pardon? To the luxury cottage.
MISTY	We'll spend just one night with Gran.
	And then we're going farther north.
SAUL	We are? Why?
MISTY	You'll come with me—to help. I will no longer just take photographs. And gawk. Like a tourist.
SAUL	Help. Help how? At your grandma's…
MISTY	No. You've taught me to do what I have to do, even if people disapprove.
	We will paint the X's off doors from the suicides.
	Clean up the yards. Hang doors that lock.
	See if we can help make the houses fit to live in—in what some of my friends call "Indian country."
	And they won't get any insurance money—ever.
SAUL	I can't. I am afraid.
	And I am afraid to go to the hospital.
	I am afraid of really angry people.
MISTY	I'll be with you.

SAUL   Those people... you want us to help in the north... may
              never thank us.

              Doesn't that bother you, Ms. Misty?

MISTY   No.

              Not much.

              Some of them might. There's at least a fifty-fifty chance.

              Drink some champagne, Mr. Saul.

                   The end.

Behind the Scenes
With Rita Shelton Deverell

From 2009–2011 Rita Shelton Deverell was the twelfth holder of Nancy's Chair in Women's Studies at Mount Saint Vincent University. This means she had the honour of being in a Chair endowed by feminist philanthropist Senator Nancy Ruth. Deverell is a broadcaster, journalist, theatre artist, and an academic.

She was living in Halifax at the historic moment when the people of Africville got an apology from the city's mayor for having destroyed their community fifty years earlier, bulldozing their church and moving their belongings in garbage trucks.

Rita has many fond memories of her time working in the artistic and cultural sectors. Chief among them was playing Dionysus in *Dionysus in '69*, where she found herself in the eye of the radical Canadian theatre boom of the '60s and '70s, and took her clothes off onstage. More soberly, she remembers being a part of the group of people that applied for and received four licences to broadcast for Vision TV from 1988–2000. Finally, she cherishes the high of wearing a name tag at Banff during Women in the Director's Chair 2006 that labelled her simply an "Artist."

The sources of inspiration for *Exit Velocity* were the front-page photographs and the news footage of 100,000 poor, trapped, and mainly Black people after Hurricane Katrina devastated the Gulf Coast of the United States in 2005.

The best thing about writing plays, states Rita, is the "If you build it they will come factor; being able to create my own vehicles at the age of sixty. It's a wonderfully satisfying sense of control." The worst thing is "How really few opportunities there are for them to come and see it, even after you've built it. Well, I can't control everything!"

Rita's next project is the production of her full-length script *McCarthy and the Old Woman*. The play is about theatre pioneer Florence James who was blacklisted during the Cold War. It will be produced in Seattle, Washington, in the very theatre building that was stolen from Florence sixty years ago. Rita has been working on Florence's story, in one form or another, for thirty years.

Obsidian Theatre, asserts Rita, has made a huge contribution and continues to do so: "I met Philip Akin when we were acting in the same show in the 1970s. He's been a supportive, ensemble kind of guy ever since. Obsidian's first production was Djanet Sears's *Adventures of a Black Girl in Search of God*. Everybody knows *now* that it is a great play; only Obsidian took the risk of knowing *then*, ten years ago. Need I say more?"

Aneemah's Spot/The Base
By Motion

voice give just granite company black theatre
OBSIDIAN ENCOURAGEMENT GLASS STRONG JET
SPACE VOICE GIVE JUST GRANITE COMPANY BLACK
THEATRE OBSIDIAN ENCOURAGEMENT GLASS
HARD STRONG SPACE JET VOICE GIVE JUST
GRANITE COMPANY BLACK THEATRE
OBSIDIAN ENCOURAGEMENT GLASS SPAC

CHARACTERS

Aneemah: Twenty-three

Wan: Twenty-four

SETTING

West-end Toronto building, 2010

PART I

ANEEMAH's spot: an apartment near the top of a high-rise over-looks the highway on the city's west end. The furniture is 1980s style, old-school, inherited from Granny: a heavy coffee table sits before a flower-print couch, faded "picture-day" photos hang on the wall. A dining table in the corner, sound equipment sits on top, a speaker bin at the side. A flat-screen TV sits on a stand in the living room.

It's mid-afternoon.

ANEEMAH stands on the balcony. She wears a short black dress and a jacket. Her feet are bare. There's a knock at the door. She walks to the door, looks out the peephole, opens it, and walks into the living room.

It's WAN. He wears a dark hoodie, a black fitted cap, a black dress shirt hangs from underneath. He stops in the hallway.

WAN   Where were you today?

ANEEMAH   Whadyou mean where I was? I was there.

WAN   Where?

ANEEMAH   At the back... in the church.

WAN   I didn't see you.

ANEEMAH   I saw you.

> *He shuts the door, leans hard on the wall.*

WAN   Yo, still can't believe this shit, guy. Fuck.

ANEEMAH   Why you left so early?

WAN   I was gonna ask you the same thing.

ANEEMAH   So how'd you know I was home then?

WAN   *(sucks his teeth, blows out a sigh)* I don't know. I just said lemme see like...

> *WAN slips off his Tims in the hallway and walks into the kitchen. He grabs a glass from the dishrack, turns the faucet on full blast, gulps down the water. ANEEMAH leans against the couch.*

I couldn't do it. I just couldn't... We was there, driving up 27, to the graveyard, right. Then I was just like, naah man... I hadda jump out the veichs, starr.

ANEEMAH   So you never went to the ground.

> *WAN shakes his head.*

WAN   Anyway. Figure the man dem be coming over, after.

ANEEMAH   Really now.

WAN   That's a next thing. Yo, I don't know what's wrong wit dese niggas right now. Just a chat pure madness, man. I'm like, yo, we're at a funeral, guy, just hold dat. But dey like, naah, dey don't give a fuck. Truss me, I can't even hear all dat right now...

ANEEMAH   Hear what?

WAN   Truss, you don't even wan know…

              WAN leans against the wall, says nothing.

ANEEMAH   Wanna drink?

WAN   You have some whites?

ANEEMAH   A sip, still.

WAN   Yeah.

              She goes to the kitchen while he moves to the couch. He unzips his hoodie as she pulls out a bottle of rum, almost empty. He yanks at a loosened tie as she grabs a glass from the cupboard. He drops on the couch. She plops the glass in front of him on a coffee table. She pours an inch of clear liquid into the glass.

              Wray & Nephew. Oh, this your man's right here?

ANEEMAH   Use to be.

WAN   Use to be, huh?

ANEEMAH   That's a whole nother story.

              WAN picks up the glass, holds it for a moment, lets a single drop fall to the carpet, his head shaking. He brings the glass to his lips, throws the rum down his throat.

              WAN puts out his hand. ANEEMAH passes him the bottle; he turns it over and drains it empty into the glass.

ANEEMAH   Felt sorry for G's moms, though.

WAN   She was wildin man… But, you know. I don't even feel nothing for that, still.

ANEEMAH   Woow, guy.

WAN   Nah. Guilt's probably licking her. How you gonna call beast
            on your youth?

ANEEMAH   It's mash up, still... but why he couldn't just get in for curfew
            though?

WAN   Doesn't matter...

ANEEMAH   See? You all always sayin dat, but differently, you're not the
            one putting up bail money, you know...

WAN   Whatever. You don't turn in your blood and flesh! If it wasn't
            for that, he wouldn't a got in beef with dem niggas when he
            was on locks... She might as well killed him...

ANEEMAH   Oh so what, she's the one who shot him now?

WAN   Why you sticking up for...

ANEEMAH   I'm not! I'm just saying... Whatever, it doesn't even matter
            now.

            ANEEMAH watches WAN as he stares into the empty glass.

            You shoulda call before you come up. I woulda told you pass,
            get a next bottle.

WAN   Call? I cut off my phone, man.

ANEEMAH   Why?

WAN   Yo, I swear, I don't know if I'm just paro right now, but... I
            swear I been hearing clicks on my phone other day...

ANEEMAH   Bwoy dem...

WAN   Dun know. And these yung heads calling me, calling me, running
            they hot lips on the phone, bout G dis and G dat. So I'm like, yo
            cut dis. I don't want nobody fe come kick off my door, seen.

ANEEMAH   F'real. Who you telling?

            ANEEMAH's cell beeps. She grabs it and checks a text.

            It's Shyanne. She's at the cemetery. "Where r u gurl?"

WAN   ...They're probably carrying his box to the hole right now.

ANEEMAH   ...Who's gonna hold up your side?

WAN   ...I don't know.

            Silence.

            *WAN reaches into his pocket, pulls out a little clear plastic bag, a
            pack of rolling papers. He grabs a magazine from the coffee table,
            unknots the bag with his teeth, begins to roll a spliff. ANEEMAH
            picks up a stick of incense and a holder from the windowsill. She
            starts to laugh.*

ANEEMAH   Know what I was thinking about today? Remember your
            rhyme when you guys did that talent show over Heights View?

WAN   What rhyme?

ANEEMAH   How it go again?

            Watch dis
            I let it off, steel hotter than hell
            Pop holes in a hood in the hood where he dwell
            Seen dark rooms, dark cells
            Niggas round me fell
            Still I'm living to tell the tale...

WAN	Mics bless like the holy grail... Wah, you rememba dem tings, ee?
ANEEMAH	What were you, like twelve, thirteen...
WAN	Something like dat...
ANEEMAH	And remember after the principal...
WAN	...lock off the school and call in security...
ANEEMAH	...drag the man dem offstage!
WAN	Holee, that was crazy!
ANEEMAH	That was jokes! Y'all bu'n down the place though... Lit'rally.
WAN	Watch that, even then we were dangerous. *(chuupss)* ...All now we coulda been out, guy. Me, your brother, G, alla we... look how much tracks we had, man? All now.
ANEEMAH	Well, y'all were kinda out I guess.
WAN	Nah, I mean like real tings, man, not just rapping round these parts, right. Just getting out... You know what I hate? Everything they have in a computer—fingerprint, my face print, my eye scan... all dat shit pops up... can't cross no border. Can't go nowheres.
ANEEMAH	Hmph... Well, everybody saw that clip y'all made for G pon Fastbook, with the freestyle and everything. Just do it.
WAN	Not without my partner, man...

WAN finishes rolling.

ANEEMAH	Anyways, you know you were better than him.
WAN	Whatever...

ANEEMAH   Maybe that's what held you back…

WAN   Wha… held me ba… Yo, you're pissing me off wit them talks, you know…

ANEEMAH   What talks?

WAN   You don't see I just put my bredren in the ground today, guy. And you're, you're coming wit dis fucken…

ANEEMAH   Relax!

WAN jumps up.

WAN   Yo… lemme just leave this place yo…

He moves toward the door.

ANEEMAH   See you? You don't change, guy.

WAN   What you talking about? What you know bout what I've changed?

ANEEMAH   From time, whenever anything get too oh deep, you run out.

WAN   Wha?

ANEEMAH   Even today, look. You run out when the man dem want talk bout tings you don't stand with, and instead of taking it like a man and speaking your mind, you bounce!

WAN   I do speak my mind.

ANEEMAH   Then do it then, instead a heading for the door…

WAN   You want me to speak my mind?

ANEEMAH   Yeah, I do.

WAN	You're sure you want me to speak my mind?
ANEEMAH	Speak it!
WAN	I think you're acting like a bitch right now, and I don't know why.
ANEEMAH	Oooh, so I'm a bitch now 'cause I'm talking truth!
WAN	You're being a bitch 'cause my boy just...
ANEEMAH	Oh, so now you tryna act like I don't know what you dealing with...
WAN	...'cause you're trying...
ANEEMAH	What I'm tryna do is show... Forget it.

There's a silence between them. WAN returns to the couch and sits back down. He holds up the spliff to AMEENAH. She waves him off.

He nudges her again.

You light it.

He grabs a lighter from the coffee table, brings the spliff to his lips, and lights. He passes the lighter to AMEENAH. She reaches over and lights the incense, then brings her face close to his ear.

Wan. I know you're in grief right, so I gave you a five-second bligh... But lemme show you something, don't ever even think bout calling me bitch again, all right, or else don't come back up in here.

WAN looks at ANEEMAH for a few moments, then leans back in the couch.

Her cell beeps again.

It's Money. He's saying if I seen you.

> *She begins to return the text. He reaches over, puts his hand over the phone, lowers it into her lap.*

WAN   It's soft I'm not there.

ANEEMAH   It's not soft... but

WAN   Tell the truth.

ANEEMAH   ...you should be there to help bury the body still...

> *WAN crosses his arms across his chest.*

WAN   Born alone, die alone...

ANEEMAH   Well, you're not exactly born alone.

> *A long beat. They sit in silence. ANEEMAH's cell beeps twice. She picks it up and slips it shut.*

> *Lights fade.*

PART II

> *The sun's going down. ANEEMAH and WAN still sit on the couch, leaned back. The incense is burned almost down. WAN's shirt is unbuttoned, revealing a white T-shirt underneath. ANEEMAH's jacket hangs over the arm of the couch. She stretches out her legs and gets up.*

ANEEMAH   You hungry?

WAN   A little bit.

ANEEMAH   A little bit, huh?

                        ANEEMAH walks into the kitchen.

WAN   I haven't really been eating, still.

                        ANEEMAH opens the fridge.

WAN   What you making?

ANEEMAH   What I'm making? I'm making sal'fish. What are you making?

                        *She takes out a pot, turns on the stove. WAN jumps up and goes
                        to the mixer on the dining table.*

WAN   Yo. Hear what I found the other day.

                        *He pulls out his cell and attaches it to the mixer. The intro to
                        "Encore," a sweet, sick anthem track blares out of the speakers.
                        Their heads nod as the beat drops. Emcee voices spit rhymes over
                        the instrumental, one hot sixteen verse flows into another. WAN
                        and ANEEMAH, in unison, rock over the hook.*

WAN/ANEEMAH   "We gon make it!!!"

ANEEMAH   Brap!

WAN   Brap!

                        *As the track fades out, ANEEMAH's head nods in the kitchen; she
                        pulls out a frying pan, turns up the burner. A new track comes
                        in, an instrumental. WAN starts to disconnect his phone.*

ANEEMAH   Yo. Pull dat up.

                        WAN reconnects and starts the beat over. It's soulful, melodic, tuff.

               Who did that? You?

WAN	Yeah.
ANEEMAH	F'real.
WAN	Hmph.
ANEEMAH	Well… didn't know you were making beats like that.
WAN	Them things from time, girl.
ANEEMAH	Now that should come out.

> *WAN stands and listens to the beat. He goes into the kitchen and leans against the wall behind ANEEMAH as she pours oil into the frying pan.*
>
> *He reaches above ANEEMAH's head and opens the cupboard, looking in.*

The flour's over there.

> *WAN reaches across the counter.*

I moved it.

WAN	So I see.

> *ANEEMAH slides a metal bowl over to WAN. He starts pouring flour in it. The beat still plays and he starts to freestyle.*

Real niggas live fast
Real niggas die young
Real niggas done wrong
Real niggas run strong
A real nigga never get to live long
But real niggas got heart
A real nigga don't run
Real niggas don't switch

Real niggas don't snitch
A real nigga got plans
Real niggas get rich
Or die
Shoot balls
Chop food
Spit rhymes
Real nigga is the truth
Till his last day shines
Then lights out…

…Fuck.

> *He pours water over the flour.* ANEEMAH *chops up some Scotch bonnet.*

So what, you not writing no more?

ANEEMAH   I don't know. Sometimes. A little bit…

WAN   Yeah. So spit one.

ANEEMAH   Why?!

WAN   Just so I can hear it, girl.

ANEEMAH   What you wanna hear it for?

WAN   Will you just do it!

> ANEEMAH *takes her time flipping through her mental Rolodex.*
>
> *She takes a breath, and flows.*

ANEEMAH   I look at you
Sunshine
Rainy dayz
See every single minute I existed

You're sooo beautiful
And don't even know it
Wish you could see what I see
A hard brotha, smoother than rocks
Jagged with soft spots
Maybe you thought
Bout what it'd be like to be with me
Ready and willing to be your beginning and ending
Filling you like water on a burning day

I'll be your mountain top
Lying on top while you climb
My valleys and peaks
Tryna conquer me
But at the same time
Loving me
Free

Yeah its crazy
Sometimes
Wondering what we did in some other lifetime...

> *She fades out and turns back to what she was doing.* WAN *lifts his head and looks at her.*

WAN   Finish that.

ANEEMAH   I don't even remember no more.

WAN   Neemah...

> *She rolls her eyes.*

ANEEMAH   I read you
               Encrypted
               Spiritually mystified by your
               Fine lines open wide
               Slipping in

Flippin off your melanin
Adrenalin rush
Finding the places that you want to be touched...

The beat stops. ANEEMAH *turns back to the pepper.*

WAN   Who'd you write that for? Dude you were seeing before?

ANEEMAH   No.

WAN nods slowly.

PART III

The oil begins to smoke.

ANEEMAH   You better get that before you burn up my house!

WAN jumps and grabs the pan off the fire, turning it down. He starts rolling dough into dumpling rounds, dropping each one into the hot oil.

WAN   I wonder...

ANEEMAH   Wonder what?

WAN   ...how much I have to make...

ANEEMAH   ...now?

WAN   A different math and thing.

ANEEMAH   Yeah.

ANEEMAH takes a pot off the stove.

Well... you know he always ate more than his share.

> *They pause in mid-air. WAN shoves the bowl away from him, it clatters against the wall. He grabs ANEEMAH's arm. She grabs his hand and pushes him off. He yanks away, stomps into the living room, pacing back and forth.*

WAN Aneemah... you're killing me right now, you know that, right... Why you doing this? What's wrong with you?

ANEEMAH Nothing's wrong with me.

WAN That's what's wrong with you! There's nothing wrong with you. Why aren't you, why aren't you, broke up, or something.

ANEEMAH I am broke up.

WAN You coulda fooled me...

ANEEMAH I'm feeling shit. I'm feeling a lot of shit.

WAN Yeah. Well, I'm feeling shit I don't even understand. I mean, you're with your bredren one second, and the next second, he's gone. Just gone. What's that?

ANEEMAH That's life.

WAN ...you know every single shit I been thru, that nigga was right beside me? I'm talking about grade school, guy. Before that.

ANEEMAH Wan, you know I was there, right?

WAN I mean, first everything...

ANEEMAH Yeah... but differently, where was that getting you though?

WAN What're you sayin to me?

ANEEMAH   Holee. Why everybody gotta be so fraud, though? Why when people die, everybody act like oh, they never was an asshole, never fucked up, never hurt nobody.

         WAN jumps up to leave, heading to the exit.

    G was all about him. Me, me, me... what the fuck, Wan. You can't see that?

WAN   Aneemah, what'd he ever do to you?

    I don't remember you complaining when man and man was burning you free weed, do I?

ANEEMAH   Yo, let me show you something, guy. Nothin's free. Ever!

         WAN's hand is on the doorknob. He stops.

WAN   Don't tell me about free, Aneemah. You can't speak to me about free...

ANEEMAH   My brother's locked up...

WAN   So what?

ANEEMAH   Because of him...

WAN   You know that's not true. Aneemah, when you gonna let that go?

ANEEMAH   Who said I'm holding onto that?

WAN   'Cause I know.

    Your brother made his own decision.

ANEEMAH   Oh, who's supposed to be running tings?

WAN   That's not the point.

ANEEMAH   You know what's the point?

           ANEEMAH moves up to WAN's *face, points her finger in his face.*

WAN   Take your hand out my face.

ANEEMAH   You're next... I'm saying you, Wan, are next in line. It's just logic.

WAN   See. You're always up in bizness that you don't understand...

ANEEMAH   ...watch, you're gonna end up...

WAN   What?!

           ANEEMAH steps closer.

ANEEMAH   My brother's locked up. G's in the ground. And what's gonna happen to you? You hafta make their destiny be your destiny, right?

WAN   What else is out here, Neemah?

           She walks back to the couch.

ANEEMAH   Tired of hearing that, man.

           Just per-petratin the cycle...

WAN   The cycle.

ANEEMAH   ...mentally.

WAN   Oh, so what. Now you go school, you on some other level and shit?

ANEEMAH	I'm not talking about no other level. I'm talking about what you think…
WAN	Think…? Aneemah, you know since this shit, man, I don't sleep. I mean, like, I don't lie down, don't close my eyes, nothing. All I do is think.
ANEEMAH	About what?
WAN	My mind's running crazy right now. Like, if I sleep, I feel…
ANEEMAH	Feel what?
WAN	Like he's coming back to get me, or something.
	Like I feel like he's the one paying for our sins right now, the wrong shit we done… It's fucked up…
ANEEMAH	What sins?
WAN	Just shit we been through, man.

ANEEMAH's cell beeps. She grabs it, reading the text on the screen.

| ANEEMAH | See! It's B… |

She throws the phone, he catches it in one hand.

How come everybody's looking for you so hard?

He reads the text, throws the phone back to her.

WAN	You don't even know half of the g'wanins, Aneemah, aright.
ANEEMAH	What, y'all think I'm really stupid or something?
WAN	Nuff things the man don't talk bout, even round you.

ANEEMAH   Whatever. Sitting in my crib, say you talking code.

WAN   Relax...

ANEEMAH   Nah man! You keep walking to the door. Where you going? Really?

           Anyways, you know what, g'wan!

           ANEEMAH rushes toward WAN, pushes him against the door.

WAN   Jus cool!

ANEEMAH   Nah, let them find you.

WAN   Who!

ANEEMAH   Oh please!

           They stop, staring at each other. ANEEMAH leaves the room, goes out on the balcony, and slams the screen door.

           WAN stands still near the door. He begins to turn the doorknob, stops suddenly. Voices in the hallway. He looks out the peephole, watches until the voices fade.

           He moves from the door, paces in the hallway. He goes back into the living room, sits on the arm of the couch.

WAN   When we were little niggas running on the block
           Then we was bigger niggas, holding up the shop
           Use to bet who'd be the first one to drop
           Who be the first pon lock, or heart stopped
           Dropped in where I fit in
           Face masks and fitteds
           Triggers under fingers
           Popping like blisters
           Twin stacks in my mattress stash

Rolling in the ride
Soundclash full blast
Megacitee hoods on this ill soundtrack
Gotta whole crew of niggas, and dey got my...

...Back...

> *WAN sits back on the couch. He leans forward, finds a roach in the ashtray. He takes up the lighter and pulls the spliff to his lips. He takes another draw, crushes it into the glass.*

I remember... when I was little, we were like, I don't know, eleven, twelve. Remember that spot they use to have in the basement? The dungeon. Yeah...

And there was this girl. What was her name again? Angela... something like that.

I go calling myself liking that. Checking for it hard, you know. This was way before that girl got ho'd out, truss me. Before all that.

I don't know, just something bout her, I liked. So I go like a ee-diot, go tell G, oh go tell her come meet me, after school, in the dungeon. Honestly... I wasn't even thinking I was gonna do nothing with her, right. I just was gonna try lyrics her up a bit...

But when this guy brings her come, he's not leaving, like.

> *The sun has gone down. ANEEMAH stares at WAN through the screen door.*

ANEEMAH   Yall battry her?

> *WAN avoids her eyes.*

WAN   Naaaah, man... She was just... just there like...

Yo, man, we've done some fucked up shit, guy.

> *The screen door opens. ANEEMAH walks back into the room. She stops at the dining table, pulls WAN's phone from the mixer. She slams it down in his lap.*

Aneemah.

> *ANEEMAH walks to the door and pulls it open.*

Don't...

ANEEMAH   Go, Wan.

WAN   No.

> *He rushes over, tries to close the door. She holds it open.*

ANEEMAH   That's fucked up, yo.

WAN   ...You don't know the half.

ANEEMAH   Probably know more than you want me to know.

WAN   What does that... what do you mean?

ANEEMAH   Little girls don't know no better!
They go looking for love in fucked up places
Find fingers in secret places
Getting invaded before their time
Never trusting the voice that hollas inside
I thought I said no, I thought I said no

WAN   Nah...

ANEEMAH   Niggas lose friends
But girls lose they innocence
And there never gets to be another first time

So we rehearse
So we can forget
Twist your spirit into fucked up poses
For those who think that you could actually love them
Hoping that you don't

WAN   Ameemah...

ANEEMAH   She couldn't even love she
But on a forever fiend for the thing she was seeking in the
Spring of her life...

WAN   Yo, I'm out...

ANEEMAH   Some people take
Feed off your energy
Get into your mind
Next you're committing felonies
Soon you have less friends than enemies
Addicted to the rush like a fiend on amphetamines
End up in a box made of concrete walls
Or in another box in a eight feet hole

WAN   ...but everybody's gotta die

ANEEMAH   But where goes them young souls
Who use to roam black roads
The stairways
The back doors
Rooftops and
Bottom floors
High-rise and townhomes

WAN   ...you're killin me...

ANEEMAH   They're gone
Leave the next set to carry on
Nothing stays the same, and

Nothing ever change…

WAN drops down on his knees.

He grips tightly to her waist.

WAN   I can hear the dirt, hitting on the top, the wood, you know. That sound… I could hear, the bulldozer, pushing the dirt. I could hear it. Just like at Chuky's funeral. Just like Powet, like Sharky, you know. I couldn't do dat again, I couldn't…

ANEEMAH stands stiff as WAN buries his face in her stomach, his shoulders shaking. She hesitantly lets her hands meet his back, his shoulders, his head. She bends down, brings her lips to his ear.

ANEEMAH   Wan. You're still here. You're still here. You don't see, you're meant to be.

WAN turns his head toward her. Their lips meet; a slow, soulful kiss. WAN rises to meet her. They hold each other, their bodies pressed against the door. They stop, their eyes locked on each other. WAN pulls ANEEMAH closer to his body, and they become wrapped in an embrace that entangles arms, thighs, breath.

In the coming darkness, the phone rings. There is a knock at the door. ANEEMAH and WAN are breathing.

The lights fade.

To black.

BEHIND THE SCENES
WITH MOTION

Also known as Wendy Braithwaite, Motion's poetry has been published by McClelland and Stewart and by Women's Press. Her work has been seen or heard at Obsidian, CBC's National Poetry Face Off, and b current's rock. paper.sistahz festival. Motion has lived all her life in Toronto, listening to Caribbean accents.

Motion's favourite gig is working as a poet/emcee. Performing puts her in motion at seminal music and spoken-word venues across Canada, the Caribbean, and the United States. They include Def Poetry Jam, the Canadian Urban Music Awards, and the International Caribbean Literary Fest. Two collections of poetry: *Motion In Poetry* and *40 Dayz*, published by Women's Press, plus a spoken-word album, *the AudioXperience*, are proud achievements of Motion's poetry career.

Another source of pride is her role as an urban-arts educator. Motion is skilled in the area of artist development and is dedicated to nurturing new talent. She has worked with young and emerging artists in groundbreaking programs such as Fresh Arts, Urban Noise, What the 411, and BLOCKHEDZ. She is currently writer-in-residence at Literature for Life.

Motion's favourite credit is as a playwright/screenwriter. She has grown artistically in the Obsidian Theatre Playwright's Unit where she first wrote *Aneemah's Spot/The Base*. The play continued its development with another staged reading at b current's rock.paper.sistahz festival.

Aneemah's Spot/The Base was inspired by a piece of visual art. "I embarked on a lengthy search for a muse, which took me everywhere from the newly relaunched AGO, to storefront galleries on Queen Street. I knew I wanted to write a piece for two people. But finding my piece happened by pure synchronicity. I had just walked off stage after performing at the *40 Dayz* book-launch party, which was held at Trane Studio, a Toronto music venue and art gallery. As I walked towards the entrance, I saw *Illuminated Whisper*. A beautiful painting by artist Jason O'Brien, *Illuminated Whisper* depicts a man and woman in deep tones with splashes of iridescence. The young man's head is bent low, as the afroed woman in profile whispers into his ear. The artwork immediately spoke to me."

For Motion the best thing about writing plays is exploring the different voices and how they interplay and intertwine with each other. The music of the voice, as a solo instrument or within a dramatic symphony, and how it relays reality, fantasy, irony, and all the facets of storytelling are aspects of writing that intrigue her.

"Rewriting, rewriting, and rewriting what I just knew was a masterpiece from the first draft!" Motion says, is the worst thing about writing plays. Both rewriting and reimagining can be difficult after that first burst of inspiration, but she declares it necessary to get closer to the play's brilliance.

Along with many of the writers in this book, a first production of a full-length version of what began as a twenty-minute play is what Motion sees as her next accomplishment. She is thankful to Philip Akin for seeing potential in her work.

The Obsidian Company, Motion concludes, "is making a space for new voices, opening the stage to theatre artists of African descent, and making a legacy by contributing to the diverse face of theatre in Canada."

BRIDGE OVER JOAN
BY RACHAEL-LEA RICKARDS

voice give just granite company black theatre
OBSIDIAN ENCOURAGEMENT GLASS STRONG JET
SPACE voice give just granite COMPANY BLACK
THEATRE obsidian encouragement GLASS
HARD STRONG space jet voice give just
GRANITE company BLACK THEATRE
OBSIDIAN ENCOURAGEMENT GLASS SPAC

CHARACTERS

Miss J: real name Joan, a forty-five-year-old homeless Black woman.

Lucy: a cocky Latina lamp post. If in human years, she'd be twenty-three.

Fez: the highway. Old and wise and easily irritated. Has been standing for at least fifty years, which is double that in people years.

Iris: a young, naive journalism student from the suburbs.

Sam: Miss J's former neighbour, in his fifties.

SETTING

Underneath the Gardiner Expressway.

MISS J	Good morning, Fez.
FEZ	Good morning, Miss J.
MISS J	And how are you today, my friend?
FEZ	Oh you know, as well as a highway can be…
MISS J	Didn't get much rest last night?
FEZ	And how much rest would one get when every few minutes tons of metal drive up your spine? Yes, I didn't think you could answer that one.
LUCY	Good morning, Miss J.
MISS J	Good morning, Lucy.
LUCY	Can you do me a favour and shut that guy up?
FEZ	How bout I shut you up.
LUCY	Ooh, real scary, Fez, what are you going to do… get up and push me… You make more noise than any rusty old engine I've heard.
FEZ	I feel my blood pressure. My blood pressure. You don't want my blood pressure to boil. *(The sound of a rumbling bridge.)* I'm not feelin good about this, someone quiet her… quiet her…

MISS J	Okay, Fez, come on, give it a rest. Relax. I don't know why you let Lucy get to you.
LUCY	Because I can.
MISS J	Lucy... if you don't stop, I'm going to...
LUCY	Okay, okay, I get it... I'll leave him alone, Miss J.
MISS J	Thank you, Lucy.
LUCY	Whateva!
FEZ	Did you hear?
MISS J	Hear what?
FEZ	They're tearing this whole place—
MISS J	Tearing what down?
LUCY	Fez, why'd you have to go there huh? Why'd ya have to upset the old lady.
MISS J	You watch who you're callin an old lady.
FEZ	Well, I think she needs to know.
LUCY	I swear, if I could walk, I'd come over there and shut your big trap!
MISS J	They can't tear this place down... it's all I have.
FEZ	Oh, you'll be all right, Miss J. I hear Sam, you know the guy who lived in the fancy wooden box just five streets over?
MISS J	Yes, Sam, I miss him.

FEZ	Well I hear that he's living in luxury. Fancy place with a washing machine and everything.
MISS J	I don't need anything fancy.
LUCY	Oh gosh, a real washing machine... Just imagine, Miss J, you'd feel like the belle at the ball.
MISS J	But I don't need to feel like the belle at the ball. Look what happened to Cinderella, she meets some man, loses her shoe, doesn't hear from the man she danced with the whole night, only until after he goes and conveniently checks out every girl in the whole damn town... Da prince was a floozy. No one ever told us what happened three years after they got married, I hear she's in therapy, but hey, you don't have to listen to me.
FEZ	Miss J, stop jokin. That's all you do. Joke, joke, joke. I'm very serious, Miss J, I heard them talking.
MISS J	You heard who talking?
FEZ	Them.
LUCY	Miss J, Fez is losing his mind. He doesn't know what he's talking about.
FEZ	Oh yes I do.
MISS J	Who was talking, Fez, who?
FEZ	The people with the hard yellow hats. The ones that drive the trucks. You know the trucks that look like they have angry frowning mouths in the front?
MISS J	Shovels, for the snow?
FEZ	Whatever. I heard them talking. You were sleeping. It was late at night. Said something about renovating the city skyline.

Said the fancy toll highway was much more practical, that the homeless situation was getting worse, that people like Sam, like you, Miss J, were making tourism plummet, and that all this… *(two beats)* all I was, *(beat)* was an eyesore.

LUCY   Well you are kinda ugly!!!

MISS J   Lucy!

LUCY   Okay, okay, you ain't that ugly…

MISS J   Don't you get it, Lucy? If they get rid of Fez, they get rid of all of us… They get rid of you too…

LUCY   Oh come on, come on… Let's not overreact now.

FEZ   Miss J is right, Lucy.

LUCY   Well, we gotta stop 'em. Do something. This is our place. Our home.

MISS J   Well they don't see it that way.

LUCY   Miss J, don't worry, everything's gonna be fine.

FEZ   Yes, Miss J, don't worry, perhaps Lucy's right.

MISS J   *(walks over to LUCY and rests her head against her pole)* Oh I hope so…

LUCY   Twelve o'clock, young girl coming in. *(LUCY and FEZ freeze and stay still.)*

IRIS   Hello? Ma'am?

MISS J   …

IRIS   Ma'am, can I please talk to you for a moment?

MISS J	Go away, there's nobody here.
IRIS	Now that's not true. I heard you laughing and talking.
MISS J	It must be the heat, perhaps heat stroke, you heard something? You heard nothing.
IRIS	But what I heard—
MISS J	What you want from me, little girl?
IRIS	Can I speak to you for a moment?
MISS J	Fine, come in, but keep your voice down, I don't need anyone else looking for room and lodging.
IRIS	Thank you.
MISS J	Well, you know it certainly isn't the house on the hills that I was banking on, but the rent is cheap and we've got at least four more months before it starts to get cold. I haven't seen you here before.
IRIS	No, I'm not from around here actually. I live about an hour out of town.
MISS J	So what's a girl like you doin in a place like this?
IRIS	Well, I'm a journalism student at the university in the city. We're doing a paper on the "disadvantaged in society," my professor said the best way to document about a certain topic is to live amongst them. And so here I am, you know… just hoping I can get some good conversation, and some good questions answered.
MISS J	Oh I see, and so you thought, "Hey, she looks disadvantaged, let me go hang with her"?

IRIS	Oh, man, that did sound bad.
MISS J	Yes, that does sound bad! so you want a couple questions answered, do you? What ever happened to young people just wanting to have a shake and a hamburger on a Saturday night? Now your idea of fun is hangin with the poor?
IRIS	So things have changed a bit. I'd be willing to give you a few dollars for your time? Perhaps a nice warm meal. How would you like that?
LUCY	"How would I like that?" How would she like that? How would you like a knuckle sandwich?

MISS J shoots a look at LUCY.

IRIS	What's the matter, ma'am?
MISS J	Nothing, girl, did you just hear something?
IRIS	No. *(takes out her pen and paper, all excited)* Should I?
MISS J	Why'd you really come down here? Are you some undercover officer or something?
IRIS	No really, I am who I say I am. But ma'am, there is help out there. Tomorrow can be brighter, look, there is a silver lining.
MISS J	You're killing me, kid. You're killing me. I'm fine, thank you, right where I belong.
IRIS	But this isn't a place for a woman to be living. Aren't you scared that someone's gonna bother you down here?
MISS J	No one bothers you on the other side of nowhere.

The song "On the Other Side of Nowhere" plays.

MISS J	Listen, I don't need your money, or your dinner. Maybe someone else will be happy to take your bribe, but I'm quite fine, thank you.
IRIS	I didn't mean to offend you.
MISS J	Yah kid, I'm sure you didn't. But I really don't think I have anything exciting to say.
IRIS	No, no, actually, I think you do. What will it take to make you talk?
MISS J	Listen here, little girl. A meal or a cup of hot cocoa isn't going to get me to spill all my hopes and dreams. *(two beats)* A meal, hot cup of cocoa, maybe pair of socks and a purple sweater, and I'll think about it.
IRIS	*(She takes off her purple sweater, takes off her socks, puts back on her shoes, and hands her socks and sweater over to MISS J.)* There, they're not brand spanking new, but they are what you wanted.
MISS J	Fair enough. I'm never one to go back on a promise. But don't expect them back.
IRIS	Thanks. I really appreciate it. I'll only be here a little while.
MISS J	What is your idea of a little while?
IRIS	A couple days, max, and then I'll be out of your hair.
MISS J	What's your name, kid?
IRIS	It's Iris.
MISS J	What kind of name is Iris?
IRIS	I don't know. It's kind of been with me, you know.

MISS J	Well, you don't look like an Iris. Maybe a Mandy, or Sandy, or even a Brandy. But Iris?
IRIS	My mother always said that the eyes are the window to the soul. Said you could always judge a person's character by the way they looked at you. When I was born, I had the largest blue-green eyes. Mom said that she could see deep to the bottom of them and swim down into my soul for hours. She called me Iris. I don't know. Mum was the artsy-fartsy type. You know the kind of person that would go to art museums and look at a black dot in the centre of a white canvas and call it art? And besides? What's in a name… who cares!

The song "What's in a Name" plays.

Enough about me, what's your name?

MISS J	Joan, but call me Miss J.
IRIS	Okay, Miss J. *(two beats)* So how long have you been out here?
MISS J	You know, *(beat)* I started to lose track a while ago. There used to be a time when days had a name, weeks had seven days, and time had a purpose. Now, it's just me and my box. It's all I got.
IRIS	But you seem so grounded, so smart.
MISS J	Well thank you, my dear, I've been waiting to hang the Harvard diploma up, I'm just waiting for the right wall to hang it on.
IRIS	And funny too.
MISS J	Can I offer you something, perhaps something warm to drink?
IRIS	Um, you have something to make warm drinks?

MISS J	No, dahling but I've been dying to say that line for years. "Can I offer you something warm to drink." Oh, oh, that and, "Well it was lovely having you, please come again."

The song "Please Come in and Stay Awhile" plays.

IRIS	Seriously, Miss J, what's your story? Do you remember the first day you got here?
MISS J	Oh yes, I do. *(two beats)* I sure do. I was married.
IRIS	And what happened? Did he die?
MISS J	You could say that. He died in my eyes. The first day I met Charlie, I knew right away that it was one of those love-at-first-sight things. Charlie had a quick wit about him. His suits always pressed, hair always greased down just right. There was a glitter in that man's eye that had all the girls going crazy. And we met, danced the night away, and the rest was history. We were married and I had a baby nine months later.
	The glitz and glamour of his lifestyle excited me, and I was sucked in by the fast life, fast cars, and fast cash. And things were good, real good. For the first five years.
IRIS	And then what happened?
MISS J	Then, he started getting crazy. Started selling things. First it was his stuff, then he started selling my stuff, and then the baby's. If I wasn't watching hard enough, he would have sold the baby too. I'm sure of it.
IRIS	So did you eventually leave him?
MISS J	After ten years, emotionally, but it took me twenty years to physically up and leave. I left him staring into the bottom of a whisky glass. I couldn't take it anymore. And I was left with nothing more than a few shirts in the closet that he couldn't

IRIS   sell cuz they were too tattered. I walked away. Walked away with not a dime in my pocket.

IRIS   What did you do?

MISS J   Stayed with friends until they got tired of me. I lost a lot of friends that year, I'll tell you that. A true test of friendship is who'll still stick around when you have nothing to offer. I lost all my friends.

IRIS   And your baby? What happened there?

MISS J   He grew up. Got married, got busy, and well, he just got busy.

IRIS   A son, you have a son?

MISS J   Yah, I have a son.

IRIS   Maybe your son can help you.

MISS J   No.

IRIS   But he's your—

MISS J   But he's my what? Son? I don't blame him. That kid spent more time being a father to his own father than a child. He spent more time wiping away my tears than playing in a sandbox. I have never seen anyone so desperate to spread their wings and fly. But he did, and I don't hate him for it. He'll always be my baby.

The song "Mama's Baby Boy" plays.

IRIS   I'm sure that I could find him.

MISS J   Iris, what don't you understand? I don't want anyone to find me. Let him be.

IRIS	Wow.
MISS J	The only thing that I have right now is this box.
	LUCY coughs.
	And of course the light from the lamppost and my trustworthy bridge that always keeps me sheltered.
LUCY	That's better!
FEZ	Shat up, Lucy.
MISS J	Yah, shut up.
IRIS	I wasn't saying anything, Miss J, I was listening. Go on.
MISS J	Sorry dahling, as I was saying, this is my home. This is my world.
IRIS	Miss J?
MISS J	Yes.
IRIS	Why did you give up?
MISS J	There's only so much noes a girl can take, Iris.
IRIS	Well haven't you ever heard the saying, "If at first you don't succeed, try and try again"?
MISS J	Oh boy, here we go again… *(gets up to move away from IRIS)*
IRIS	There is truth to it, Miss J, and if you give up on wishing then what do you have? *(starts singing "When You Wish Upon a Star" in MISS J's ear)*

MISS J	You know what, kid? As much as I know your intentions are good, I just don't think this is gonna work. I'm not good interview material. And besides, I'm getting tired.
IRIS	Okay, fair enough. Enough questions for today.
MISS J	Thank you. Gosh, you really have me working for a sweater that's not even a designer.
IRIS	And how would you know that's not a designer?
MISS J	I know what's hot and what's not. I walk up and down the main street enough, and this, girlfriend, is not a designer

The song "You're Either Hot or You're Not" plays.

IRIS	Miss J, just one more thing.
MISS J	*(two beats)* Yes, Iris.
IRIS	I can tell you were pretty when you were younger and I just think with a little help, we could make you look so pretty again.
MISS J	For what?
IRIS	Oh, I don't know, didn't you ever just want to feel pretty for yourself?
MISS J	Getting pretty, I never had time for. I forget what pretty looks like.
IRIS	Will you let me… *(MISS J doesn't resist.)*

> *IRIS pulls a couple of bobby pins our of her hair and upsweeps MISS J's kinky hair into a neat upsweep. She grabs a tissue from out of her bag and wipes the dirt off of her face. She then gets lipstick out of her purse and attempts to put it on MISS J's lips, but MISS J interrupts.*

MISS J	Hey, you might have germs; I don't know where your hands have been.

IRIS and MISS J look at each other and then smile, IRIS continues by putting on some lipstick.

IRIS takes a mirror out of her pocket and puts it in front of MISS J.

(softly takes the mirror into her own hands and looks at herself and begins to cry) I haven't seen this face in so long.

IRIS	You are beautiful.
MISS J	I left this girl behind so many years ago. I don't need your help. *(MISS J wipes the lipstick off with her arm and it streaks across her cheek.)* That girl died a long time ago. She's dead, do you get it? She's dead.
IRIS	Okay, Miss J, I was only trying to help.
MISS J	I don't need your help.
IRIS	You know, maybe I should go. Perhaps I'm causing more harm than good.
MISS J	...
IRIS	I'll go, thank you. I've taken up enough of your time. Goodbye, Miss J. See you tomorrow.

IRIS exits. The lights go down, leaving the stage only dimly set. MISS J walks over to the mirror that she threw on the ground and picks it up one more time, looks in it, smiles, and puts her hand over her mouth to hide her happiness.

MISS J	*(talks to herself in the mirror)* Would you like something warm to drink?

The song "On the Other Side of the Nowhere" plays.

FEZ   They're coming, Lucy, they're coming.

LUCY   Let her be, Fez, just for tonight, let her sleep.

Lights to black.

SCENE 2

Lights up.

LUCY   Hey Miss J, you aren't actually considering having that girl come back here, are ya?

MISS J   A promise is a promise, Lucy.

LUCY   Well you must really like her.

MISS J   And why would you say that?

LUCY   You've rearranged the furniture. Made things look all formal and stuff.

FEZ   Sounds like someone is a bit jealous.

LUCY   Me, jealous? Come on, why would I be jealous? Look at me, I'm fabulous. I turn on, off, I've got killa curves. Who wouldn't want to be me? That girl ain't got nothin on me.

FEZ   You're afraid Miss J likes her better than she likes you.

LUCY   That's not possible, right Miss J?

MISS J   Right, Lucy, I mean look at you. You're fabulous!

FEZ   Miss J.

MISS J	Yes, Fez?
FEZ	I was thinking.
MISS J	Thinking is always good.
FEZ	See, there you go again. Joke, joke, joke.
MISS J	Fez, come on, I'm sorry, I should know better. What is it that you're thinking about?
FEZ	She could help you, the skinny gangly girl. She could help.
MISS J	And how could she do that?
FEZ	She could help save our home. Be nice to her, Miss J.
MISS J	You know, Fez, you do have a point. She did say she was a journalist. She could help me write to someone important.
LUCY	I bet she knows some of those people who walk really fast in the mornings with suits and running shoes on. You know the ones who eat sushi on the lawns down by the lake?
MISS J	Maybe, Lucy, maybe
FEZ	Don't underestimate her, Miss J. She may be tiny, but it only takes a small speck of dirt to get under an eyelid to make the biggest men jump around like fools.
LUCY	He's right, Miss J, in fact I thought…
MISS J	Go on, Lucy, what were you saying. You thought what?
FEZ	Pssst! Miss J. The gangly girl, the gangly girl!
MISS J	Good morning, Iris, I wasn't expecting you so early.

IRIS	I brought you a double frappaccino with whipped cream and caramel.
MISS J	A what?
IRIS	A double frappaccino with whipped cream and caramel.
MISS J	No thanks, I don't like Italian food.
IRIS	Miss J, it's coffee, don't you like coffee?
MISS J	Then why didn't you just say coffee?
IRIS	I'm sorry, I thought you knew what's hot and what's not!! *(laughs)*
MISS J	Did you have a side order of sass for breakfast?
IRIS	No, cheese omelette, and I brought you some too.

> *The song "Frappalino Cappaccino, What the Heck is That!" plays.*

> MISS J *takes the cheese omelette, squats near her box, and starts to eat very fast. She is unaware that* IRIS *is watching her.*

Miss J.

MISS J	Yes! *(realizes she's eating way too quickly and forgetting her manners)* I just didn't want it to get cold.
IRIS	*(sits down next to her and sips on her coffee)* Miss J, don't worry, I'll bring you more. *(hands her the coffee she brought for her)*
MISS J	Thank you, Iris. No one has ever bought me something so lovely.

Owww! It's too hot!

| IRIS | Oh man, I should have warned you. |

| MISS J | *(two beats)* No, I'm sorry. *(two beats)* Thank you. I can't remember the last time anyone has bought something so nice for me. |

| IRIS | Oh come on, Miss J, it's no big deal, it's only coffee. I'm sorry Miss J, you're welcome. |

Okay, it's your part of the deal. It's question time.

| MISS J | I suppose. I've just eaten your omelette and drank your coffee, guess yes would be the right response. |

| IRIS | Guess that sounds about right. |

| MISS J | Okay, kid, go on, what do you want to know? |

| IRIS | Did you ever fall in love again? |

| MISS J | Oh come on, kid. |

| IRIS | No really, Miss J. Did you? |

| MISS J | I did. His name was Sam. He lived five blocks over from here. But he's gone now so it doesn't matter. |

| IRIS | Where is he? |

| MISS J | He lives in a fancy apartment with a real washing machine. |

| IRIS | Tell me more. |

| MISS J | Sam, he taught me so much with such little words. He taught me about the sky, the stars. He showed me that every night, nature made its own television show. That the wind made the sweetest music. But he was getting old, you know. Sam was at least fifteen years older than me. And as time passed, I could tell that the cold and the ground was getting to him. So when |

he got the opportunity to leave, he did. And just like my son, I don't blame him.

IRIS   Did you love him?

MISS J   I did. He loved me for who I was and what I brought to his life. He expected nothing and I expected nothing either. Some nights, we just sat together without even a word spoken. We didn't need to. We were connected.

IRIS   Do you ever want to see him again?

MISS J   Yes. But it wouldn't be the same if I saw him now.

IRIS   Why not? You could start a new life, be his wife, fall in love.

MISS J   I'll always love Sam, and I don't have to be with him to love him.

IRIS   But what about all this lovey-dovey stuff?

MISS J   Iris. Can you do something for me?

IRIS   Sure Miss J, anything, what would you like?

MISS J   Did you hear they're tearing this place down?

IRIS   Uh, I did know about it.

MISS J   Do you think you can help us, Iris?

IRIS   Help us?

MISS J   Help me, help me.

IRIS   I told you I'd help you from the first day, Joan. I promised I would. It's part of the reason I came here, to be honest. But Miss J, there's something I have to tell you.

MISS J	Oh thank you, Iris, thank you.
IRIS	Miss J, I honestly want to help you. I do. But my father… *(beat)* have you ever heard of Beatsburg and Brothers?
MISS J	Can't say I have.
IRIS	It's the family business. It's been in our family for over sixty years.
MISS J	But what does that have to do with me?
FEZ	*(muffling his screams)*
IRIS	It has a whole lot, Miss J. That's the thing.
	(IRIS's phone rings.) Hello? Yes, Daddy. No, I'm sorry, I know you were expecting me. Yes, I know that it's an important night. I'm just with *(pauses)* Sharon, from school. We're just catching up on some homework. I don't know where the time went. I'll see you in an hour. Okay. Bye. Listen, Miss J, I have to—
MISS J	Why didn't you tell your father the truth?
IRIS	Miss J, he wouldn't understand.
MISS J	Wouldn't understand why you're hanging out with some homeless lady?
IRIS	Yes, I mean, no… I mean, he just wouldn't understand.

The song "Things Like That Never Happen to Us" plays.

Miss J, Daddy is in a world of his own, so busy trying to get business deals met that he barely even knows I'm in journalism school, that I exist these days. All he cares about is that the family business does well.

MISS J	Are you coming back? Will I see you again?
IRIS	Yes, of course I will, I promise. I want to help, Miss J. I just need some time to talk to Daddy. Just give me some time.
MISS J	Don't make promises you can't keep, Iris.
IRIS	I'm sorry, Miss J, I have to go, I just don't have much choice.
MISS J	Everyone has a choice.
IRIS	I have to go.
MISS J	Well, it's perfect timing anyways because I was expecting a call from the queen. She's been anxiously waiting for me to return her phone calls and I just haven't had the time.

> *IRIS looks sadly at MISS J and runs back quickly and gives MISS J a kiss on the cheek—IRIS exits.*

FEZ	Aaaaah! Oh no, oh no. *(bridge starts to rumble)* Do you know what this means?
MISS J	Calm down, Fez, calm down.
LUCY	Calm down, Fez! Breathe, breathe!
FEZ	The gangly girl's father... is... is...
MISS J	Is who, Fez?
LUCY	If he doesn't calm down, he's gonna croak. I swear he's gonna kick da bucket!
FEZ	He's one of the men with the yellow hats.
MISS J	No, I don't believe you.

FEZ	It's true. I see the name on the side of the trucks. Very clearly. It says "Beatsburg and Brothe" the r and the s at the end has been rubbed off. But I am sure. The gangly girl's father is the man in the yellow hat… guess the other one is his… brother.
LUCY	Why didn't she tell you sooner?
MISS J	Sometimes people do things without thinking, Lucy. Like the time when that young Samson kid decided to put his tongue against your pole in the dead of winter. I'm sure he didn't mean to get stuck. I'm sure he didn't mean to cause a crowd. I'm sure he didn't mean to have his mother rush all the way down here and miss five hours of work. Sometimes people just do things without thinking.
FEZ	Miss J, I have to be honest. It's time for you to go.
MISS J	Go where?
FEZ	Every night the sound of jackhammers and steel machines gets louder and louder. It's not safe here for you anymore, Miss J. It's time for you to go.
LUCY	He's right, Miss J. You need to go live in a fancy place. Find Sam. He always had a thing for you, and from what you told Iris, you had a thing for him too.
MISS J	I've got to do something. If Iris isn't going to help me, I'm sure someone will. I'm going to take a walk over by city hall. Someone's got to listen to me. Someone.

The song "I'm a Citizen Too" plays.

FEZ	Yes, Miss J, perhaps you're right, take a walk over to city hall. And if someone doesn't see you, wait, wait as long as you can, they can't ignore citizens forever.

LUCY	Yah, Miss J, do what the old man tells ya. Sit and wait, someone's gotta listen to you.
MISS J	You're right, guys. I deserve to be heard. I'll be back as soon as I can. Now don't fight.
FEZ & LUCY	We won't, Miss J.

MISS J exits.

FEZ	I haven't said this to you before, and I know I have given you a hard time, but... I love you, Lucy
LUCY	I love you too, old man. I love you too.

Lights to black.

SCENE 3

Lights up.

IRIS	*(Walks back on stage, which is covered with smoke. All that remains is a pile of rubble.)* Miss J? Miss J?
MISS J	Why did you lie to me, Iris? Why couldn't you tell me the truth?
IRIS	I'm sorry, Miss J. I'm sorry. I wanted to help. I tried to prove to my father that there was reason to keep the old bridge, your home. But he didn't see it my way. When I went to go and meet him, I tried to convince him to come and meet you. I told him that the minute he looked into your eyes that he'd have to put the construction on hold. Where were you, Miss J? Where were you?
MISS J	What do you mean?

IRIS	My father said he actually took the time to come down here, and he saw nothing. Says all he saw was a shopping cart and box. Why did you leave?
MISS J	Oh God. I left to go to city hall. Fez? Lucy? They're gone.
IRIS	Who's gone, Miss J?
MISS J	My friends. They're all I had.
IRIS	What friends, Miss J? You said you were alone. Daddy said he didn't see you or anyone and he said he couldn't wait any longer. I'm so sorry, Miss J. I'm so sorry.
	Miss J, please let me help you.
MISS J	Iris, I know your intentions were good. I know you wanted to help. But please, just let me be.
IRIS	I'm sorry, Miss J. I'm sorry. *(exits)*
	The song "You're a Whisper in the Wind" plays.
	MISS J *sits, crying.*
SAM	Joan, my precious Joan.
MISS J	Sam?
SAM	I heard they took your home away.
MISS J	It's all gone, everything is gone.
SAM	The most important thing is that you're fine.
MISS J	Thank you, Sam.

SAM	Joan, we weathered the cold together. And I'm sorry I left you. I am. Let's never be apart again, and besides *(pause)* have you heard?
MISS J	Heard what?
SAM	I have a real washing...
MISS J	I know, a real washing machine. I missed you, Sam, washing machine or not.

Soft muffles from LUCY are heard under the rubble.

LUCY	*(louder, but SAM can't hear)* Get me outta here!
SAM	Miss J, let's go. Come with me.
MISS J	*(speaks to SAM)* Sam, I will, but can you just give me a couple of minutes?
SAM	Sure, I know it's hard. Take your time and say goodbye, I'll give you time to say goodbbye. *(exits)*
MISS J	*(walks over to rubble)* Lucy? Is that you?
LUCY	No, it's the other lamppost you've been talking to for the past five years. Of course it's me!
MISS J	My God, you're alive.
FEZ	Miss J.
MISS J	Fez, my Fez, is that you? You made it too?
FEZ	Alive and kicking, baby. They got rid of most of me, but they can't kill my spirit.
MISS J	Spirit never dies. You're right—

LUCY	So your Sammy Sam came back for ya. He loves ya, Miss J, can't ya see it?
MISS J	So it seems, Lucy, so it seems. I'll be back for you in the evening. I promise. Sam! I'm coming!
FEZ	We'll be here, Miss J. We'll be waiting.
LUCY	No, Fez, we'll be running a marathon, of course we'll be here. We got a choice?
FEZ	Listen here, Lucy, don't start with me.
LUCY	Real scary, Fez, real scary.
FEZ	My blood pressure, my blood pressure.
MISS J	Guys, give it a rest!

Behind the Scenes
with Rachael-Lea Rickards

Rachael-Lea is an actor, writer, and journalist. She has been in several editions of *'da Kink in my hair* and *I am Not a Dinner Mint*, is a writer for *Sway* magazine, and a theatre critic for www.tdotexposed.com.

Rickard's favourite credits include taking on the responsibility of writer, performer, and any other role needed for *I am Not a Dinner Mint*. She is also proud of being a touring cast member of *da Kink in my hair* for Mirvish Productions, Hackeny Empire-London, and the New York Fringe Festival.

Rachael-Lea's goal in the Obsidian Playwrights Unit was to write something on her own after having so much success as a co-writer. She was motivated to write in an unfamiliar way, to stretch her possibilities as a writer.

The best thing about writing plays for Rickards is the freedom. "I am not afraid to offend and I find when I write for theatre, I feel brave. It's an organic process that cannot be repeated in any other form. It's breathing life into stories and putting them on stage. How magical."

And the worst thing about writing plays for Rickards is the familiar issue of writer's block, the fear of not getting it right. Even worse for Rachael-Lea is the greater fear that she might get it right.

Rickards is working towards a full musical version of *Bridge Over Joan*. She plans to accomplish this through workshops of the play. She appreciates that Obsidian Theatre Company "gives us a voice, gives us spaces to tell our stories," going on to say that "Obsidian gives us a sense of pride and the encouragement to continue in our journeys as writers."

You can find Rachael-Lea at *Sway* magazine and at www.allthingsrachael-lea.com.

Rita Shelton Deverell, C.M., Ed.D. is a theatre artist, broadcaster, university professor, and television producer/director/writer. She has supervised and hosted over 2,000 current affairs programs, and since 2005 written four theatre pieces and eight TV drama titles. From 2009–2011 Dr. Deverell was the Nancy's Chair in Women's Studies at Mount Saint Vincent University in Halifax. She has written widely on the role of women, persons with disabilities, visible minority, and Aboriginal creators in media. Deverell has received numerous awards, including two Geminis, the Black Women's Civic Engagement Network Leadership Award, and was appointed to the Order of Canada in 2005 for her pioneering work in broadcasting, notably the founding of Vision TV and mentoring her Aboriginal successor at APTN National News. She has served on several boards of directors, among them Obsidian Theatre Company, Creative Women's Workshops Association, and OCAD University.